Quick & Easy
New Style Japanese Cooking

Better Home Publishing House

Contents

Tofu and Others ■

Soups ■

Rice and Pasta ■

How to Use the Book

The following standards are used in this book:

1 Tbs = 15cc

1 tsp = 5cc

Microwave oven = 500 watt machine is used in this book (If your microwave power is greater or less, please adjust your cooking time accordingly.)

Utensil marks = Each recipe has a utensil mark (chopping board; skillet; pan; toaster oven; microwave oven). This tells you which utensils are needed to make the recipe.

Ingredients = For native Japanese ingredients, both the Japanese and English names are written, for example, mochi (rice cake). Some pictures and explanations are included on p.96 for your reference.

Spicy Fried Chicken

Tabasco and pepper give a spicy kick to this chicken recipe. Thinly slicing the chicken diagonally saves oil and time and only a skillet is necessary.

20 min.
455 kcal

- ■ Ingredients (2 servings)
8¾oz／250g chicken breast
A ┌ ⅓oz／10g garlic
  │ ⅓ to ½ tsp salt and Tabasco
  └ pinch of pepper
2 Tbs flour
7oz／200g frozen potatoes
  pinch of salt
oil for deep-frying
lemon and watercress

❶ Cut the chicken diagonally into the larger pieces. Grate the garlic. Rub A into and all over the chicken to season, then set aside for 5 to 6 minutes.

❷ Coat the chicken with flour.

❸ Deep-fry the potatoes in 370°F ／180°C oil and sprinkle with salt.

❹ Deep-fry the chicken until crisp and golden brown. Transfer the chicken and potatoes to a plate and garnish with lemon and watercress.

Note: Curry powder, 7-spice pepper powder(p.96), or chile powder can be used instead of Tabasco.

Menu: Green Salad
       Quick Clam Chowder(p.85)
       French Bread

Curry Chicken and Mushrooms

15 min.
439 kcal

■ Ingredients (2 servings)
7oz／200g chicken breast   ¼ onion
A ┌ ⅙ tsp salt   3 Tbs white wine
  │ pinch of pepper   3 Tbs heavy cream
  └ 1 tsp curry powder   pinch of salt and pepper
3½oz／100g shimeji mushrooms   2 Tbs vegetable oil

❶ Cut the chicken diagonally into the larger pieces. Season with A. Tear the shimeji into small clusters and thinly slice the onion.

❷ Heat 1 Tbs of oil in a skillet, place the chicken skin side down first and pan-broil both sides until nicely browned. Remove from heat and set aside.

❸ Add the remaining 1 Tbs of oil and sauté the onion. When tender, add the shimeji and sauté a bit longer.

❹ Pour the wine into the skillet, then put the chicken back. Reduce the heat to low, cover and braise for 2 to 3 minutes. Add the heavy cream, then season with salt and pepper to taste. Turn off the heat when it starts to bubble.

Menu: Cabbage and Corn Salad (p.53)／Spinach Soup／Bread

Ingredients (2 servings)

7oz／200g　　chicken thigh
　pinch of salt and pepper
　1 Tbs　　flour
½　　onion
6　　string beans
⅓oz／10g　　garlic

A ┌ ½ (approx.7oz／200g)
　│　unseasoned canned tomato
　│　and liquid
　└ 50cc　　white wine

1　　bouillon cube
1 Tbs　　vegetable oil
pinch of salt and pepper

❶ Cut the chicken diagonally into the larger pieces. Season with salt and pepper, then coat with flour.

❷ Cut the onion into ⅜-inch/ 1-cm-wide wedges and the string beans into manageable pieces. Mince the garlic.

❸ Heat the oil in a skillet. Sauté the garlic until aromatic. Slide the chicken into the skillet skin side down and pan-broil both sides until golden brown. Add the onion and string beans and continue to sauté. When the onion is tender, add A and the crushed bouillon cube. Crush the tomato with a flat wooden spoon. Cover and bring to a boil, then reduce the heat to low and braise for 2 to 3 minutes. Season with salt and pepper to taste.

Menu:　Chinese Cabbage and Apple Salad(p.59)／Julienne Vegetable Soup／French Bread

Braised Chicken with Tomato

20 min.
312 kcal

In this dish, all the ingredients are briefly cooked with unseasoned canned tomato. If desired, 1 tsp of sugar can be added to reduce the acidic taste of the tomato.

Chicken with Miso Sauce

■ Ingredients (2 servings)

7oz／200g   chicken thigh

⅙ tsp   salt

pinch of pepper

1   negi(long onion)

A
- 1 Tbs   sugar
- 1½ Tbs   miso
- 2 Tbs   sake
- ½ Tbs   soy sauce

1 Tbs   vegetable oil

❶ Butterfly cut the chicken by slicing into the thick part and season with salt and pepper. Cut the long onion into about 3-inch /8-cm-long and ³⁄₁₆-inch /5-mm-wide strips.

❷ Put A in a bowl, mix well, wrap, and heat for about 30 seconds in a microwave oven.

❸ In a skillet, heat 1 tsp of oil. Sauté the long onion and remove. Add 2 tsp of oil, place the chicken skin side down, and pan-broil over moderate heat until crisp. Turn over, slightly reduce the heat, cover, and cook until heated

The thick, rich taste of miso sauce also makes an excellent base for boiled konnyaku jelly, broiled daikon radish, and pork for shabu-shabu.

through.

❹ Cut the chicken into manageable sizes and transfer to a plate. Pour ② over them and top with the sautéed long onion.

Menu: Kiriboshi-Daikon Salad(p.74)／Tofu and Egg Puff Soup(p.84)／Steamed Rice

Menu: Quick Simmered Lettuce and Prawns (p.60)／Daikon with Umeboshi (p.54)
／Miso Soup (p.80)／Steamed Rice

20 min.
263 kcal

Grilled Chicken with Salt and Sake

Using high quality chicken such as Jidori maximizes the flavor of this dish. The simple recipe requires only a sprinkling of salt and sake before grilling, but produces a full, delicious taste.

■ Ingredients (2 servings)

10½oz／300g	chicken thigh
1 Tbs	sake
⅔ tsp	salt
3½oz／100g	pumpkin
2 to 3 pieces	eringi mushrooms
1	sudachi (or lemon)

❶ Cut the pumpkin into ⅜-inch／1-cm-thick wedges, wrap and heat for about 2 minutes in a microwave oven. Then grill with the eringis until browned. Tear the eringis into manageable strips.

❷ Evenly slice the thick part of the chicken open. Sprinkle the sake and half the salt over the meat side.

❸ Grill the chicken on the meat side first for 4 to 5 minutes, then turn over, sprinkle with remaining salt and continue grilling until the skin is crisp. Cut into serving-sized pieces.

❹ Arrange the chicken and vegetables on a platter and garnish with sudachi wedges.

Note: You should salt the chicken just before you begin grilling, so that it stays juicy.

■ Ingredients (2 servings)

10½oz／300g   chicken thigh

1   negi (long onion)

6   shishi-togarashi (small sweet green pepper)

½ to 1   dried red pepper

½ Tbs   vegetable oil

A ┌ ½ Tbs   sugar
  │ 3 Tbs   sake
  └ 2 Tbs   each soy sauce, mirin and water

❶ Seed the red pepper and chop into fine rings. Cut the chicken diagonally into bite-sized pieces. Cut the long onion into chunks. Combine A.

❷ Heat the oil in a skillet. Add the chicken, and brown nicely on both sides. Halfway through, add the long onion and shishi-to-garashi, and brown them lightly.

Menu: Microwave-Warmed Tofu (p.70)／Crisp Soybean Sprouts(p.63)／Miso Soup(p.80)／Steamed Rice

Braised Chicken, Nanban Style

12 min.
322 kcal

❸ Add A and the red pepper. Cover with a drop-lid, reduce the heat and braise until the broth is almost gone.

By beautifully browning the chicken before braising it, you can get an attractive finish as well as a rich and full taste .

■ Ingredients (2 servings)

10½oz／300g   chicken thigh

    pinch of salt and pepper

4inch／10cm   negi(long onion)

2 Tbs   ponzu-joyu(lemon-soy mixture)

❶ Evenly slice the thick part of the chicken open and season with salt and pepper. Coarsely mince the long onion, then place in the ponzu-joyu.

❷ Pan-broil the chicken skin side down first in a dry skillet until browned, then turn over and continue pan-broiling until heated through.

❸ Cut the chicken into manageable sizes. Pour the long onion-and-lemon-soy mixture over the chicken. Serve with your choice of 7-spice pepper powder or Chinese chile oil.

Chicken with Lemon-Soy Sauce

15 min.
222 kcal

The secret of this recipe is to cook the chicken skin until it is very crisp. The flavor of the long onion steeps into the sauce, producing a rich taste.

Menu: Bean and Lotus Root Salad(p.64)／ Toasted Shirataki (p.73)／ Instant Clear Soup(p.85)／Steamed Rice

Menu: Sautéed Komatsuna and Harusame (p.44) / Kiriboshi-Daikon Salad (p.74) / Soup / Steamed Rice

15min.
235kcal

Chilled Wonton

Cucumber is the main ingredient of this dish. Its refreshing and crisp taste enhances the appetite.

■ Ingredients (2 servings)

3½oz／100g   ground chicken

½   cucumber

A ⌈ ½ Tbs   mayonnaise
  ⌊ pinch of salt and sesame oil

15 to 16   square wonton skins

B ⌈ ponzu-joyu (lemon-soy mixture)
  ⌊ pinch of red pepper flakes

❶ Cut the cucumber into 1⅙-inch／3-cm-long julienne strips, then toss with a pinch of salt (optional). When they have wilted, squeeze lightly to drain the water.

❷ Place the ground chicken and A in a bowl. Add ①.

❸ Place a spoonful of ② on each wonton skin. Wet the edges of the skin lightly, and fold into a triangle. Press to seal.

❹ Boil the wontons in plenty of boiling water (it is easier to handle if you boil them in two batches). When the wontons float up to the surface, plunge into cold water. Serve with B as a dipping sauce.

The mayonnaise both combines the ingredients and adds body to the dish.

■ Ingredients (2 servings)

4 pieces (5⅗oz／160g)
        pre-sliced chicken breast
pinch of sake and salt
  1 Tbs   cornstarch
1   cucumber
6   cherry tomatoes
A [2 Tbs   mayonnaise
  [1 tsp   wasabi paste(p.96)

❶ Remove the tendon from the chicken, cut into diagonal bite-sized pieces and sprinkle with sake and salt. Dredge lightly in cornstarch. Boil, then plunge into ice water and drain in a colander.

❷ Cut the cucumber into diagonal chunks by rotating it 90° after

Menu: Steamed Tofu, Chinese Style (p.68)／Chicken Soup *／Steamed Rice

Cornstarch Chicken

12min.
224kcal

each cut. Cut the cherry tomatoes in half. Toss them with the chicken and place on a plate.

❸ Combine A. Serve with A as a sauce.

*To make an easy chicken broth, season the chicken-boiling liquid with sake, soy sauce and salt and add vegetables of your choice.

■ Ingredients (2 servings)

4 pieces (5⅗oz／160g)
        pre-sliced chicken breast
A [pinch of salt and pepper
  [1 Tbs   sake
5¼oz／150g   broccoli
2oz／60g   pizza cheese, grated
pinch of salt and pepper
¼   lemon
cooking paper, butter

❶ Remove the tendon from the chicken, cut into diagonal bite-sized pieces and season with A.

❷ Divide the broccoli into small florets.

❸ Spread a little butter on the center of the cooking paper and place the chicken and broccoli on

Steamed Chicken with Cheese

10min.
226kcal

it. Sprinkle with salt and pepper, top with cheese and twist the ends of the paper to close.

❹ Put the packets on a plate and heat for about 5 minutes in a micro-

If you prepare up to step ③ ahead of time, you can serve a hot dish in only 5 minutes.

wave oven (about 3 minutes per serving). Serve with lemon wedges.

Marinated Pork Sauté

This fancy Italian dish is very easy to cook.

15min.
489kcal

■ Ingredients (2 servings)

4 slices (7oz／200g)　pork loin, medium thinly sliced

pinch of salt and pepper

A
- 2　basil sprigs
- ⅙oz／5g　garlic
- 2 Tbs　olive oil
- 2 Tbs　white wine

<Garnish>

1　eggplant

1　tomato

pinch of salt and pepper

1 Tbs　olive oil

❶ Coarsely mince the basil and garlic, then combine A. Pound the meat lightly and sprinkle with salt and pepper. Pour A over the meat and let stand for 5 minutes.

❷ Cut the eggplant into thin slices and the tomato into round slices.

❸ Heat the oil in a skillet. Pan-broil ②, then sprinkle with salt and pepper. Remove.

❹ Pan-broil the meat until done.

For best results, place the meat in the marinade and set aside for a while. This gives the flavor time to absorb and also keeps the meat tender.

Garlic and Ginger Pork Sauté

15min.
395kcal

■ Ingredients (2 servings)

7oz／200g　pork loin, thinly sliced

A
- 1 Tbs　each soy sauce, sake, oyster sauce and fresh ginger juice
- ⅙oz／5g　garlic

2 tsp　sesame oil

10　Chinese lettuce leaves

1　cucumber

⅓oz／10g　sliced almonds

❶ Cut the cucumber into thin strips. Toast the sliced almonds in a dry skillet for 2 to 3 minutes until crisp.

❷ Grate the garlic. Combine A, add the meat and rub well.

❸ Heat the sesame oil in a skillet and pan-broil the meat.

❹ Arrange the vegetables and meat on a plate. Sprinkle with toasted almonds. To eat, wrap the meat and cucumber in a lettuce leaf and eat it with your hands.

Menu:　Bean Sprouts with Chinese Chile Sauce (p.62)／Simmered Beans／Miso Soup (p.80)／Steamed Rice

Menu: Pumpkin Salad with French Dressing (p.48)／Soup／Steamed Rice

Pork Sauté with Garlic

15 min.
535 kcal

Cutlets are easy to prepare and cook, and can
be used in a great variety of dishes.

■ Ingredients (2 servings)
2 cuts (7oz／200g)
    port loin for pork cutlet

A ⎰ ⅓oz／10g   garlic, grated
    2 Tbs   sake
    1 Tbs   soy sauce

1 Tbs   flour
⅓oz／10g   garlic, thinly sliced
1 Tbs   butter
<Garnish>
1¾oz／50g   carrot
1   bell pepper
3½oz／100g   onion
1½ Tbs   vegetable oil

❶ Prepare the meat (see below) and pound lightly, then steep in A for about 5 minutes. Cut the carrot and bell pepper into julienne strips. Thinly slice the onion.

❷ Wipe the meat dry and lightly coat with flour.

❸ Sauté the garnish vegetables in 1 Tbs of oil and sprinkle with salt and pepper(optional). Remove.

❹ Sauté the garlic in ½ Tbs of oil and 1 Tbs of butter over low heat until lightly browned. Remove the garlic and pan-broil the meat over moderate heat until browned. Turn over, then reduce the heat a little, and cook until heated through.

Cut the white tendon between meat and fat at 2 to 3 places to keep the meat from shrinking or bending backwards while cooking.

14

Ingredients (2 servings)

2 cuts (7oz／200g)
    pork loin for pork cutlet
    pinch of salt and pepper
2 slices   canned pineapple
   ┌2 Tbs   pineapple liquid
A│1 Tbs   Worcestershire sauce
   └50cc   water
pinch of salt and pepper
1 Tbs   vegetable oil
<Garnish>
spinach, sautéed in butter

❶ Cut the pineapple into small cubes. Cut the tendon of the meat at 3-4 places, pound lightly and sprinkle with salt and pepper.
❷ Heat the oil in a skillet, pan-broil the meat until cooked through and transfer to a plate

Menu: Cabbage and Corn Salad (p.53)／Soup／Bread

Pork Sauté with Pineapple

12 min.
470 kcal

The sweet and sour taste of pineapple makes a good match for the pork.

with the garnish. Briefly sauté the pineapple and place on the meat.
❸ Pour A into the skillet. Thicken the sauce a little by mixing with the leftover drippings. Season with salt and pepper to taste and pour over the meat.

Pork Sauté with Mustard Dressing

12 min.
551 kcal

The highlights of this dish are the well-matched sour flavor of ground mustard and the mild taste of heavy cream.

Ingredients (2 servings)

2 cuts (7oz／200g)
    pork loin for pork cutlet
    pinch of salt and pepper
1 Tbs   vegetable oil
   ┌1 Tbs   butter
A│50cc   heavy cream
   └½ Tbs   stone-ground
    mustard and lemon juice
pinch of salt and pepper
<Garnish>
parsley, cherry tomatoes

❶ Cut the tendon of the meat at several places, pound lightly and sprinkle with salt and pepper.
❷ Heat the oil in a skillet and pan-broil the meat until heated through. Transfer to a plate.
❸ Wipe the remaining oil from the skillet. Add A. Once it reaches a boil, season with salt and pepper to taste. Pour over the meat and garnish with parsley and cherry tomatoes.

Menu: Steamed Mushrooms with Garlic(p.51)／Pasta／Soup

Menu: Chingensai with Mustard Dressing(p.45)／Chinese Cabbage Soup／Steamed Rice

Sautéed Pork and Yam with Salt

15 min.
322kcal

In this recipe you can opt for a crisp texture by using briefly sautéed nagaimo, or create a more tender dish by using well-sautéed nagaimo. The white nagaimo makes a striking dish.

White cloud ear mushroom has a very plain taste, so it goes well as an ingredient in soup, salad, dressing, etc.

■ Ingredients (2 servings)

5¼oz／150g   pork loin, thinly sliced

A ⌈ ⅙ tsp   salt
     pinch of pepper
   ⌊ 1 Tbs   sake

7oz／200g   nagaimo(Chinese yam)

⅙oz／5g   white cloud ear mushrooms
(or cloud ear mushrooms)

4inch/10cm   negi (long onion)

B ⌈ 2 Tbs   sake
   ⎮ ⅓ tsp   sugar and salt
   ⌊ pinch of pepper

1½ Tbs   vegetable oil

❶ Cut the meat into bite-sized pieces, then season with A.

❷ Peel the yam and cut into about ³⁄₁₆-inch/5-mm-thick rounds. Soak the cloud ear mushrooms in water until soft and large. Cut off any tough parts, then cut into bite-sized pieces. Cut the long onion into thin diagonal slices. Combine B.

❸ Heat ½ Tbs of oil in a skillet. Sauté the meat and remove.

❹ Add 1 Tbs of oil and sauté the yam for 2 to 3 minutes. Add the long onion and cloud ear mushrooms, sauté a bit longer, then put the meat back in the skillet. Add B and stir to coat.

Ingredients (2 servings)

5¼oz∕150g		pork loin, thinly sliced
⅙ tsp	salt	
1 Tbs	sake	
2	eggplants	
2	cucumbers	
½ tsp	salt	
4inch/10cm		negi (long onion), minced
¼ tsp		tou ban qiang(Chinese chile sauce)
A ⌈ 1½ Tbs		Worcestershire sauce
⌊ 2 Tbs	sake	
1½ Tbs		vegetable oil

❶ Cut the eggplant in half, then into 6 pieces. Cut the cucumber into pieces about the same size as the eggplant. Sprinkle salt

Sautéed Eggplant and Cucumber

20 min.
298 kcal

This dish is a great way to use up leftover vegetables.

over both, and squeeze lightly after about 10 minutes.

❷ Cut the meat into bite-sized pieces and sprinkle with salt and sake. Combine A.

❸ Heat the oil in a skillet. Sauté the long onion and Chinese chile sauce. When they flavor out, add the meat and sauté.

❹ Add ①. When the eggplant is tender, add A and stir to coat quickly.

Ingredients (2 servings)

5¼oz∕150g		pork loin, thinly sliced
⅙ tsp	salt	
1 Tbs	sake	
4⅕oz∕120g		tou miáo (young green pea sprouts)
2 (1¾oz∕50g)		small red bell peppers
A ⌈ 1 Tbs		oyster sauce and sake
⎸ 1 tsp		soy sauce
⌊		pinch of salt and pepper
2 Tbs		vegetable oil

❶ Cut the meat into bite-sized pieces and season with salt and sake. Combine A.

❷ Cut the tou miáo into 2inch∕5 cm lengths and the bell peppers into ³⁄₁₆-inch/5-mm-wide strips.

Sautéed Pork with Tou Miáo

10 min.
330 kcal

Soybean sprouts are available if you don't have tou miáo.

❸ Heat the oil in a skillet. Sauté the meat until it is no longer pink. Add the bell peppers first, then the tou miáo and sauté briefly.

❹ Add A and mix well until everything is coated.

Menu: Liang Pan Style Mushroom Salad (p.51)∕Wakame Soup∕Steamed Rice

Menu: Simmered Daikon and Tofu-Puff(p.54) ／ Vegetable Salad(p.65) ／ Miso Soup ／ Steamed Rice

Enoki Mushroom Hamburger

This healthy alternative to the standard burger uses lots of enokis. The simple preparation requires only cutting a few ingredients. The crisp texture of enokis makes this recipe a big favorite.

20 min.
265 kcal

■ Ingredients (2 servings)

3½oz／100g		ground pork
A	½	egg
	1 tsp	soy sauce
	½ tsp	fresh ginger juice
	1½ Tbs	cornstarch
3½oz／100g		enoki mushrooms
5 to 6		scallions
1 Tbs		vegetable oil
grated daikon radish		

❶ Cut off the root cluster of the enoki and cut into approx.1⅛ inch/3cm lengths. Chop the scallion into fine rings.

❷ Put the ground meat and A in a bowl and mix well. Add ① and mix further.

❸ Divide into 4 portions and form into patties.

❹ Heat the oil in a skillet, and pan-broil the burgers until heated through. Transfer to a plate with a mound of grated daikon radish. Serve with 7-spice pepper(p.96) and soy sauce, if desired .

Make the burgers about ⅜inch/1cm thicknesses. If they are too thick, they will take much longer to cook. The best method for grilling is to grill one side over moderate heat until browned, then turn over, cover and cook for about 4 minutes over low heat.

■ Ingredients (2 servings)

7oz／200g   pork tender-
loin, chunk

pinch of salt and pepper

2 Tbs   flour

2   potatoes

1   onion

2 Tbs   butter

A ⌈ 1   bouillon cube
  ⌊ 2 Tbs   white wine

❶ Cut the onion into approx.¼-inch/7-mm-wide strips.Cut the potatoes into rounds about the same thickness as the onion and soak in water.

❷ Cut the meat into approx.⅓-inch/8-mm-thick pieces.Season with salt and pepper, then dust with flour.

Pork and Potato Layer

15 min.
409 kcal

❸ Melt the butter in a skillet, then pan-broil the meat on both sides. Place the potatoes and then the onion on top of the meat, and add enough water to just cover everything. Add A, cover and simmer over moderate heat until the potatoes soften.

❹ Adjust the seasoning with salt and pepper and sprinkle with minced parsley.

■ Ingredients (2 servings)

12 slices (approx.7oz／200g)
pork ham,wafer-thin slices

6   shiitake mushrooms

A ⌈ 1½ Tbs   sake and soy sauce
  │ ⅙oz／5g   garlic
  ⌊ ½ tsp   tou ban qiang(Chinese
        chile sauce)

2 Tbs   flour

1   egg

2 Tbs   vegetable oil

6   bamboo skewers

❶ Grate the garlic. Combine A in a bowl and mix. Rub the meat well in it and let stand for about 5 minutes. Remove the shiitake stems and cut in half. Beat the egg.

❷ Skewer 2 slices of the meat

Mexican Glazed Pork Kabobs

20 min.
338kcal

Soaking the meat in egg before grilling gives it a soft, juicy finish.

and 2 pieces of the halved shiitakes, and dust with flour.

❸ Heat the oil in a skillet. Dredge the skewered meat and shiitakes in the beaten egg and pan-broil until heated through.

Menu: Eggplant and Bell Pepper with Sesame Dressing(p.56)／Lettuce Soup ／Steamed Rice

Sesame Dressing

Grilling the beef enhances the sesame-soy flavor of this dish.

20 min.
597kcal

■ Ingredients (2 servings)

2 steaks(10½oz／300g)　beef

A ⎰ 1½ Tbs　each sugar, soy sauce and sesame oil
⎰ ¼ tsp　salt
⎰ ½　negi (long onion)
⎰ 1 Tbs　roasted white sesame seeds
⎰ pinch of 7-spice pepper

5¼oz／150g　sweet potatoes

6　shishi-togarashi (small sweet green pepper)

❶ Mince the long onion. Coarsely chop the sesame. Combine A.

❷ Cut the tendon of the meat at several places, pound lightly and soak in A for 5 minutes.

❸ Cut the sweet potatoes into ⅜-inch/1-cm-thick slices, and soak in water to remove the starch. Wrap and heat for about 4 minutes in a microwave oven, then broil with the shishi-togarashi on a grill. Transfer to a plate.

❹ Grill the meat until browned. Turn over and evenly brush the remaining dipping sauce on the meat and continue grilling. Cut into manageable pieces and transfer to the plate.

Menu:　Chingensai with Mustard Dressing(p.45)／Wakame Seaweed Soup／Steamed Rice

Beef with Sautéed Vegetables

12 min.
313 kcal

■ Ingredients (2 servings)

1 steak (5¼oz／150g)　beef

⅙ tsp　salt

½　onion

1　red bell pepper

1　green bell pepper

3½oz／100g　shimeji mushrooms

⅙oz／5g　ginger

A ⎰ 1 Tbs　sake and soy sauce
⎰ ½ Tbs　oyster sauce

½ tsp　coarsely ground black pepper

1½ Tbs　vegetable oil

❶ Cut the onion and bell peppers into ⅜-inch/1-cm-wide strips. Separate the shimeji into small bunches. Thinly slice the ginger. Combine A.

❷ Cut the tendon of the meat at several places, pound lightly and sprinkle with salt. Heat ½ Tbs of oil in a skillet, and pan-broil the steak until done to your liking. Remove and cut into ½-inch/1½-cm-wide pieces

❸ Clean the skillet, add 1 Tbs of oil and sauté the ginger until aromatic. Add the remaining vegetables and sauté over high heat.

❹ Put the meat back in and sprinkle with coarsely ground pepper. Add A and toss to coat.

Menu:　Tofu and Egg Puff Soup(p.84)／Bread

Ingredients (2 servings)

7oz／200g	beef, medium thinly sliced
⅙ tsp	salt
pinch of pepper	
1 Tbs	vegetable oil

<maitake sauce>

1¾oz／50g	maitake mushrooms
½ Tbs	butter

A ⎡ ½ Tbs butter
  ⎢ ½ Tbs flour
  ⎣ 80cc milk

pinch of salt and pepper

<garnish>

3½oz／100g	spinach

❶ Blanch the spinach and cut into manageable lengths. Sauté in butter and transfer to a plate.

❷ In a bowl, blend the flour and milk of A well. Add the butter and heat, uncovered, for about 1⅔ minutes in a microwave oven. Mix well and season with a pinch of salt and pepper to taste.

❸ Divide the maitakes into small clusters. Sauté briefly in ½ Tbs of butter. Sprinkle with a pinch of salt and pepper and add to ②.

❹ Sprinkle salt and pepper over the meat. Pan-broil in a skillet and transfer to the plate. Pour ③ over the meat and spinach. Serve.

Menu: Green Vegetable Salad／Cheese Gyoza Soup(p.79)／French Bread

Sautéed Beef
with Maitake Mushroom Sauce

Maitake sauce gives a lift to ordinary sautéed meat.

15 min.
333kcal

The key to making a smooth white sauce using a microwave oven is to add the milk little by little to keep it from becoming lumpy at the beginning.

15 min.
263kcal

Menu: Pumpkin and Sweet Potato Salad(p.48)／Soup／Bread

Ingredients (2 servings)

7oz／200g   beef, medium
               thinly sliced
⅙ tsp   salt
pinch of pepper
1 Tbs   vegetable oil
<wine sauce>
¼   onion, thinly sliced

A ⎡ 100cc   red wine
  ⎢ ⅓ tsp   bouillon powder
  ⎣ 70cc   water

pinch of salt and pepper
1 tsp   butter
<garnish>
string beans, boiled
shimeji mushrooms

❶ Briefly sauté the boiled string beans and shimeji in butter and transfer to a plate.

Sautéed Beef in Wine Sauce

❷ Sprinkle salt and pepper over the meat. Broil and transfer to the plate.

❸ Place the onion and A in the skillet without cleaning it. Simmer the onion with the meat drippings until half the liquid has been absorbed. Season with salt and pepper to taste, add the butter and remove from heat. Pour the sauce over the meat.

Ingredients (2 servings)

7oz／200g   beef, medium
               thinly sliced
⅙ tsp   salt
pinch of pepper
1 Tbs   vegetable oil
<wasabi sauce>
6   watercress

A ⎡ ½ tsp   wasabi paste(p.96)
  ⎢ ½ tsp   soy sauce
  ⎢ 80cc   dashi stock(p.96)
  ⎢ pinch of pepper
  ⎣ ½ tsp   cornstarch

<garnish>
3½oz／100g   nagaimo
                (Chinese yam)
1 tsp   butter

❶ Sprinkle salt and pepper over the meat. Cut the watercress into 1⅛inch／3cm lengths. Cut the

Sautéed Beef with Wasabi Sauce

20 min.
297kcal

nagaimo into ³⁄₁₆inch／5mm rounds and brown in the butter. Set aside.

❷ Heat the oil in a skillet. Pan-broil the meat and set aside.

❸ Put A into the same skillet, mix well and place on moderate heat. When it comes to a boil and the sauce slightly thickens, add the watercress and remove from the heat. Pour over the meat.

Menu: Green Salad／Fruits／Soup

Creamed Beef and Vegetables

20 min.
356 kcal

Use Japanese sake instead of wine to get a milder taste.

■ Ingredients (2 servings)

3½oz／100g   beef round,
    medium thinly sliced

A ⎡ pinch of salt and pepper
  ⎣ ½ Tbs   flour

1   potato
½   onion
1   bell pepper
1 Tbs   vegetable oil
3 Tbs   sake
60cc   heavy cream

❶ Cut the potato into approx.¼ inch／7mm matchsticks. Soak in water to remove the starch and drain in a colander. Cut the onion and bell peppers into similarly sized pieces. Cut the meat into thin strips and coat with A.

❷ Place the potatoes and onions on a plate and sprinkle with a pinch of salt (optional). Wrap and heat for about 3 minutes in a microwave oven.

❸ Heat the oil in a skillet. Sauté the meat until it changes color. Add the vegetables and sauté briefly. Add the sake, cover and braise for 2 to 3 minutes.

❹ Add the heavy cream and simmer for 1 to 2 minutes. Season with a pinch of salt and pepper(optional) to taste.

■ Ingredients (2 servings)

7oz／200g   beef,
                  wafer-thin slices

1   dried bay leaf

1   tomato

3 to 4   watercress

A ⎡ 3 Tbs   rice vinegar
    ½ tsp   salt
    pinch of pepper
  ⎣ 3 Tbs   vegetable oil

❶ Combine A for the marinade and mix well.

❷ Put the bay leaf into plenty of boiling water. Boil the meat slices one by one very briefly, drain in a colander and soak them in the marinade.

❸ Cut the tomato into thin wedges and the watercress into

Menu: Cheese-Topped Grilled Yam and Okra(p.46)／Bean Soup (p.79)／Bread

Marinated Beef Salad

In this recipe, the beef only needs a very short time to marinate; however, the result is a full-flavored dish.

manageable lengths.

❹ Toss ② and ③ quickly and transfer to a plate.

■ Ingredients (2 servings)

8 thin slices   beef round

2 (2oz／60g)   sweet pickled
                  cucumbers

1/2   celery stalk

4 slices   cheese

A [pinch each of salt, pepper and nutmeg]

1 Tbs   vegetable oil

lettuce leaves,cherry tomatoes

❶ Slice the lettuce leaves into thin strips and arrange on a platter with the cherry tomatoes.

❷ Cut the pickles in quarters lengthwise. Remove the strings from the celery stalk, then cut into similarly sized pieces. Cut the cheese slices in half. Spread out the meat, sprinkle with A and lay

Rolled Beef

first the cheese, then the pickles and finally the celery on top. Roll up the meat.

❸ Heat the oil in a skillet. Place the meat rolls with the ends tucked under and leave until the ends stay tucked. Then, pan-broil, rolling them.

❹ Arrange on the platter. Serve with mustard, if preferred.

Menu: Mild Pumpkin Salad (p.49)／Soup／Bread

20 min.
384 kcal

Cheese-Breaded Beef

The meat used in this recipe is thin, so it fries quickly. If you use very fine bread crumbs, you can get a Vienna schnitzel-style finish.

■ Ingredients (2 servings)
4 (5⅗oz／160g)   beef,
            medium thinly sliced
    pinch of salt and pepper
    1 Tbs   flour
<egg water>
½ egg+ ½ Tbs water
<batter>
1oz／30g   bread crumbs
2 Tbs   powdered cheese
oil for deep-fry
<garnish>
2 to 3   pleat lettuce leaves
¼   lemon

❶ Blend the bread crumbs and the powered cheese.

❷ Lightly pound the meat to flatten. Sprinkle with salt and pepper and slightly coat with flour. Dip in the egg water and roll in the batter.

❸ Pour ³⁄₁₆inch／5mm of oil in a skillet and pan-fry the meat over low heat 320°F/160°C until both sides are nicely browned.

❹ Garnish with lettuce and lemon.

³⁄₁₆inch／5mm of oil is deep enough to fry for this recipe, so you can use a skillet.

26

Ingredients (2 servings)

5¼oz／150g   beef loin,
           thinly sliced
  pinch of salt and pepper
  1 Tbs   sake
3½oz／100g   nira(Chinese leek)
1   tomato
A ⌈ ½ Tbs   sugar
   ⌊ 1 Tbs   soy sauce
1 Tbs   vegetable oil
1 Tbs   sesame oil

❶ Cut the nira into 1⅛inch/3cm lengths and the tomato into 6 to 8 wedges. Cut the meat into bite-sized pieces. Season with salt, pepper and sake. Combine A.

❷ Heat the oil in a skillet and sauté the meat over high heat.

Sautéed Beef with Nira and Tomato

15 min.
299 kcal

❸ When the meat turns whitish, add the nira and tomato. Sauté briefly and drizzle first A, then the sesame oil over everything.

Nira, or Chinese leek, is a very nutritious ingredient. The key to this recipe is to sauté briefly over high heat to keep the nira crisp.

Ingredients (2 servings)

7oz／200g   beef loin, thinly sliced
7oz／200g   shirataki filaments
1¾oz／50g   scallions
A ⌈ 60cc   sake
  │ 2 Tbs   sugar
  ⌊ 3 Tbs   soy sauce
2   eggs

❶Roughly chop the scallions. Briefly parboil the shirataki to extract the harsh taste, and cut into manageable pieces.

❷Put A in a skillet, bring to a boil and add the meat and shirataki. When the meat turns whitish, add the scallions.

❸When the scallions are tender, break the eggs and slip them in.

Easy Sukiyaki

13 min.
515 kcal

This sukiyaki style recipe requires only a skillet.

Cook for 20 to 30 seconds and remove from heat.

Menu: Mushrooms with Daikon(p.50)／Pickles／Steamed Rice

Sea Bream with Cream Sauce

20 min.
345kcal

*Fresh unsalted salmon, fresh unsalted codfish, etc. can be substituted for sea bream.

■ Ingredients (2 servings)
2 fillets (7oz／200g)　sea bream*
　⅙ tsp　salt
　pinch of pepper
1　small tomato
4　string beans
50cc　white wine
1　dried bay leaf
100cc　heavy cream
pinch of salt and pepper

❶ Sprinkle salt and pepper over the fish and set aside for 10 min..
❷ Cut the tomato into approx.⅜ inch/1cm cubes. Wrap the string beans, heat for about 30 seconds in a microwave oven and cut diagonally.
❸ Wipe the fish dry and put in a skillet with the white wine and the bay leaf. Cover and braise over moderate heat. When the fish is cooked through, remove and transfer to a plate.
❹ In the same skillet, add the heavy cream and simmer until the sauce has reduced by half. Add ② and cook briefly. Adjust the seasoning with salt and pepper and pour over the fish.

Steamed Sea Bream with Umeboshi

When cooking only with a microwave oven, it is best to use very fresh fish.

15 min.
141 kcal

■ Ingredients (2 servings)
2 fillets (7oz／200g)　　　1 (⅔oz／20g)　umeboshi
　sea bream　　　　　　　(pickled Japanese plum p.96)
　⅙ tsp　salt　　　　　　　┌2 Tbs　sake
5¼oz／150g　cabbage　　A│1 tsp　soy sauce
⅙oz／5g　ginger　　　　　 │1 tsp　mirin(p.96)
3　perilla leaves　　　　　 └pinch of pepper

❶ Sprinkle salt over the fish and let stand for 10 minutes.
❷ Thinly slice the cabbage. Cut the ginger into julienne strips. Cut the perilla leaves in the same way and soak in cold water to keep crisp. Seed the umeboshi and tear by hand into desired-sized pieces.
❸ Combine A. Spread out the cabbage on serving plate. After patting dry the fish, place it on the cabbage. Pour A over the fish. Place the umeboshi and ginger on top of the fish, wrap and heat in a microwave oven for about 3 minutes per serving. Pile the perilla leaves on top.

■ Ingredients (2 servings)

2 fillets (7oz／200g)   fresh codfish*, unsalted

pinch of salt and pepper

½ Tbs   white wine

½   onion

3½oz／100g   shimeji mushrooms

A
- 1   egg
- 4 Tbs   milk
- 2 Tbs   mayonnaise
- 1 tsp   stone-ground mustard
- ½ Tbs   flour

½ Tbs   butter

❶ Sprinkle salt, pepper and wine over the codfish. Thinly slice the onion and spread on a heat-proof baking dish. Place the codfish on it, wrap and heat in a microwave oven for about 4 minutes.

❷ Separate the shimeji into small clusters. Beat A with whisk.

❸ Place the shimeji on ①. Pour A over everything, and dot with butter.

❹ Bake in a toaster oven for 6 to 7 minutes until browned.

*Sea bream or fresh salmon can be used for this recipe as well.

Codfish au Gratin, Souffle Style

15 min.
283 kcal

The secret to the souffle style of this recipe is in the egg and a small amount of flour. Stone-ground mustard used as a hidden ingredient gives a lively taste to this dish.

■ Ingredients (2 servings)

2 fillets (8⅖oz／240g)
    red sea bream

A ⎡3 Tbs   each sake, soy
             sauce and water
  ⎣1 Tbs   sugar and mirin

⅓oz／10g   ginger, thinly sliced

1¾oz／50g   burdock

6   scallions

⅔oz／20g   salted wakame(p.96)

½ block (5¼oz／150g)   grilled tofu

❶ Cut the vegetables, wakame and tofu into desired sizes.Soak the wakame in cold water.

❷ Bring A(combined) and the ginger to a boil. Add the fish and ladle the cooking liquid over them. Skim off any scum, cover with a drop-lid and simmer over moderate

Menu: Eringi and Mitsuba Salad with Nori(p.50)／Miso Soup(p.80)／Steamed Rice

Simmered Fish

18 min.
269 kcal

In this recipe, the fish stock is used as a broth in which to cook the garnishes.

heat for 6 to 7 minutes. Set aside.

❸ Add 100cc water to the broth and cook the burdock for 3 to 4

minutes. Add the grilled tofu, wakame and scallions one by one and cook briefly.

■ Ingredients (2 servings)

2 fillets   marlin
    pinch of salt and pepper

3½oz／100g   mixed Chinese
             vegetables, frozen

1½ Tbs   vegetable oil

A ⎡1 Tbs   each sugar, soy sauce
   ⎪   and rice vinegar
   ⎪½ tsp   bouillon powder
   ⎣50cc   water

B ⎡½ Tbs   cornstarch
  ⎣1 Tbs   water

❶ Sprinkle salt and pepper over the fish. Combine A and B separately.

❷ Heat 1 Tbs of oil in a skillet. Pan-broil the fish on both sides until heated through. Set aside.

❸ Add the remaining oil to the

Marlin with Vegetables

15 min.
266 kcal

This quick and easy recipe makes good use of frozen vegetables, and is really useful when you don't have much preparation time.

skillet and sauté the vegetables.

❹ Add A and heat until boiling.

Sprinkle in the dissolved corn-starch. Pour over the fish.

Menu : Cabbage Stalk with Sesame Dressing(p.52)／Beef and Daikon Soup(p.82)／Steamed Rice

15 min.
234 kcal

Steamed Salmon with Oyster Sauce

The key to this recipe is to pour the hot sesame oil over a generous amount of finely sliced long onions.

■ Ingredients (2 servings)

2 fillets (7oz／200g)   fresh salmon

   ¼ tsp   salt

   pinch of pepper

A ⎡ ½ Tbs   oyster sauce
   | 1 tsp   sake
   | 1 tsp   cornstarch
   ⎣ ½ tsp   soy sauce

3   shiitake mushrooms

⅓oz／10g   ginger

8inch／20cm   negi (long onion)

½ to 1 Tbs   sesame oil

❶ Cut the salmon into bite-sized pieces and sprinkle with salt and pepper. Combine A in a bowl and add the salmon. Let it steep well to absorb the flavor.

❷ Remove the shiitake stems and diagonally slice the caps into 3 to 4 pieces. Cut the ginger into julienne strips. Cut the long onion into 2inch/5cm lengths and cut each of them in half lengthwise. Remove the core and cut into fine strips. Soak in cold water and drain.

❸ Alternate the salmon with the shiitakes on a platter and put the ginger on top. Wrap loosely and heat in a microwave oven for 6 to 7 minutes (4 minutes per serving).

❹ Arrange the salmon and shiitakes on serving plates and pile plenty of rinsed long onions on top. Heat the sesame oil in a small pan and pour over the long onions.

■ Ingredients (2 servings)

2 fillets   salmon, lightly salted

½ (3½oz／100g)   lettuce

1 tsp   vegetable oil

pinch of salt

⅔oz／20g   garlic

A ⎡ ½ Tbs   sesame oil
   ⎣ ½ Tbs   vegetable oil

B ⎡ 1 Tbs   rice vinegar
   ⎣ ½ tsp   soy sauce

❶ Cut the lettuce into large pieces. Thinly slice the garlic. Heat the oil in a skillet and sauté the lettuce until wilted. Add a pinch of salt and 100cc of water. When it comes to a boil, drain in a colander and set aside.

❷ Sauté the garlic with A until lightly browned. Remove and set

Sautéed Salmon with Garlic

15 min.
273 kcal

aside.

❸ Place the salmon in the skillet and pan-broil on both sides.

Finally, add B and leave as is for a while to let the flavor steep in. Arrange ①,② and ③ on a plate.

Broiled Marinated Salmon

20 min.
223 kcal

This dish is delicious either served right away, or after 2 to 3 days. If you serve it later, reduce the amount of salt to sprinkle over the fish.

■ Ingredients (2 servings)

2 fillets (7oz／200g)   fresh salmon

¼ tsp   salt

3½oz／100g   maitake mushrooms

12   shishi-togarashi(small sweet green peppers)

A ⎡ 1 Tbs   sugar
   | 1 Tbs   soy sauce
   | 3 Tbs   rice vinegar
   ⎣ 2 Tbs   sake

❶ Sprinkle salt over the fish and let stand for 5 minutes.

❷ Divide the maitakes into the larger clusters. Shallowly score the shishi-togarashi.

❸ Combine A in a bowl.

❹ Wipe the fish dry, broil on a grid

and soak in A. Broil the vegetables and soak in A for 10 minutes,

turning them over once halfway through cooking.

Menu: Taipei Style Green Salad (p.44)／Daikon with Umeboshi (p.54)／Miso Soup (p.80)／Steamed Rice

20min.
249kcal

Broiled Marlin with Miso-Mayo Dressing

Marlin is an ingredient which can come in handy year-round. Even when using a cheaper, leaner variety of marlin, the mayonnaise gives it a moist, delicious flavor.

■ Ingredients (2 servings)

2 fillets (7oz／200g)   marlin

  ⅙ tsp   salt

A ⎧ 2 tsp   sake

  ⎪ ½-odd Tbs   miso

  ⎨ 2 Tbs   mayonnaise

  ⎪ 4inch／10cm   negi (long onion)

  ⎩ ⅓oz／10g   ginger

<garnish>

3   bell peppers

1   celery stalk

  pinch of salt and pepper

❶ Sprinkle salt and sake over the fish and let stand for 10 min..

❷ Mince the long onion and ginger and mix with A.

❸ Cut the bell peppers and celery into manageable pieces. Broil on a grid, and sprinkle with salt and pepper.

❹ Wipe the fish dry and broil on a grid for 3 to 4 minutes. When seventy percent done, turn it over. Evenly spread ② on the fish and continue to broil for 3 to 4 minutes until the topping turns light brown.

Note: Spotted mackerel, fresh salmon, or chicken can be used instead of marlin.

■ Ingredients (2 servings)

7oz／200g   fresh bonito, edible raw

A
1 tsp   fresh ginger juice
⅙oz／5g   garlic, grated
1 Tbs   soy sauce
1 Tbs   rice vinegar

½   onion
½   cucumber
¼ sheet   yaki-nori (p.96)
½ kabosu (p.96) or ¼ lemon

❶ Cut the bonito block lengthwise into approx.²⁄₇-inch／7-mm-thick pieces and steep in A for about 15 minutes.

❷ Thinly slice the onion, soak in cold water and drain. Cut the cucumber into thin strips and combine with the sliced onion.

Menu: Microwave-Warmed Tofu (p.70)／Nira and Enoki with Sesame-Miso Dressing (p.63)／Instant Clear Soup (p.85)／Steamed Rice

Fresh Bonito Marinade

20min.
160kcal

This makes a nice alternative to Bonito Tataki (lightly grilled bonito with condiments). It can also be served as a bonito bowl by placing it on hot steamed rice.

❸ Arrange ① and ② on a plate, top with thinly sliced yaki-nori and serve with kabosu or lemon as a garnish.

■ Ingredients (2 servings)

7½oz／200g   bonito, edible raw
pinch of salt and pepper
⅔oz／20g   garlic
½   onion
2   scallions
1½ Tbs   vegetable oil

A
2 tsp   lemon juice
1 Tbs   soy sauce

❶ Cut the bonito into ⅜-inch／1-cm-thick pieces, sprinkle with salt and pepper and let stand for about 5 minutes. Thinly slice the garlic.

❷ Cut the onion and scallions into manageable pieces.

❸ Heat the oil in a skillet and sauté the garlic over low heat until

Broiled Bonito with Garlic

10min.
264kcal

lightly browned. Set aside.

❹ Turn up the heat and briefly pan-broil the bonito on both sides until the center is rare or slightly reddish in the center. Take care not to overcook to keep the bonito moist. Arrange the bonito and onion on a plate and sprinkle with garlic and scallions. Pour A over everything.

Seafood

Green Salad／Simmered Sweet Potatoes with Sugar／Miso Soup
(p.80)／Steamed Rice

Sautéed Horse Mackerel with Vinegar-Soy Dressing

20min.
342kcal

The aromatic flavor of the roasted sesame
and the tart taste of vinegar-soy dressing
stimulate the appetite.

■ Ingredients (2 servings)
4 fillets (7oz／200g)
   horse mackerel
  pinch of salt
  ½ Tbs   sake

A ⎡ ⅓oz／10g   grated bread
             crumbs
    2 Tbs   roasted white
  ⎣   sesame seeds

B ⎡ 1 Tbs   soy sauce
  ⎣ 1 Tbs   rice vinegar
  2 Tbs   vegetable oil
<garnish>
  3   lettuce leaves
  ½   celery stalk
  ½ sheet   yaki-nori (p.96)

❶ Cut the lettuce into the thick-er sized strips and the celery into rectangles.

❷ Sprinkle salt and sake over the fish and set aside for 1 to 2 minutes.

❸ Without wiping the fish, coat with A on both sides. Heat the oil in a skillet and begin to pan-broil the fish meat side first over moderate heat, then brown well on both sides. Combine B and evenly pour all over the fish.

❹ Roughly crumple up the yaki-nori into pieces by hand, mix with ① and arrange as a garnish.

■ Ingredients (2 servings)

2 fillets (7oz／200g)
    yellowtail

A
  1 Tbs   sake and soy sauce
  ⅙oz／5g   ginger, grated
  ¼ tsp   7-spice pepper(p.96)

7oz／200g   daikon radish

B
  1 Tbs   rice vinegar
  1 tsp   sugar
  pinch of salt
  pinch of julienne yuzu citron rinds

pinch of scallions, for decoration

Menu: Sautéed Potato and Onion (p.47)／Green Salad／Miso Soup／Steamed Rice

Broiled Yellowtail with Daikon

20min.
289kcal

❶ Combine A. Steep the fish in A for about 10 minutes.

❷ Grate the daikon radish, drain lightly and mix with B.

❸ Pat the fish dry and broil on both sides on a grill until well browned. Baste 1 to 2 times while broiling.

❹ Transfer the fish to a plate and generously pile ② on top.

The contrasting tastes of the hot 7-spice pepper and the gentle sweet and sour daikon radish match very well in this recipe.

■ Ingredients (2 servings)

2   sardines, large whole
¼ tsp salt, pinch of pepper
1 Tbs   flour
1 Tbs   vegetable oil
2 slices   cheese, a kind that melts well
2 eggs + 1 tsp   minced parsley
<garnish>
cabbage, tomatoes

Sautéed Sardines with Cheese

20min.
398kcal

❶ Cut the cabbage into manageable pieces. Wrap and heat in a microwave oven for about 1½ minutes. Sprinkle with a pinch of salt and pepper (optional), then arrange with tomatoes on a plate.

❷ Open the sardines by hand*, sprinkle with salt and pepper and coat with flour.

❸ Heat the oil in a skillet and brown the sardines well on both sides. Wipe off the excess oil.

❹ Place the cheese on the sardines and slide in the beaten egg. Cover and steam for 2 minutes.

*To open the sardines, gut and place your thumbs on the backbone. Open the body by sliding your thumbs along the backbone. Then remove the backbone from the meat.

The combination of mackerel and butter produces this full-flavored, enchanting dish. Serve hot from the skillet.

■ Ingredients (2 servings)
2 fillets (8⅗oz/250g)
   mackerel
   1 Tbs   flour
1   negi (long onion)
 2 Tbs   butter
pinch of soy sauce

❶ Bone the fish and cut diagonally into bite-sized pieces. Lightly dust with flour. Diagonally cut the long onion into thin slices.
❷ Melt 1 Tbs of butter in a skillet. Place the fish skin side down, then pan-broil on both sides until cooked through. Transfer to a plate. Wipe the skillet.
❸ Melt the remaining 1 Tbs of butter in the skillet. Briefly sauté the long onions. Place them on top of the fish. Pour the soy sauce over the fish.

Menu: Simmered Yam and Kelp (p.46)／Vegetable Salad (p.65)／Instant Clear Soup (p.85)／Steamed Rice

Butter Sautéed Mackerel

13min.
433kcal

■ Ingredients (2 servings)

2 fillets (7oz／200g)　mackerel

A
- 1 Tbs　　each miso, sugar, sake, mirin and soy sauce
- 3 Tbs　　water
- 1 tsp　　garlic and ginger, minced
- ½　dried red pepper, fine rings

3½oz／100g　　garlic shoots

pinch of dried red pepper threads (if available)

❶ Make a few slashes on the fish skin. Cut the garlic shoots into about 1½inch／4cm lengths.

❷ Place the fish in A(combined), wrap and heat in a microwave oven for about 3 minutes. Pour the drippings over the fish.

❸ Add the garlic shoots, wrap

Korean Style Mackerel with Miso Sauce

and heat for another 5 minutes.

❹ Arrange the fish and garlic shoots on a plate. Heat the remaining drippings uncovered in a microwave oven for about 2 to 3 minutes to thicken a little. Pour over the fish. Sprinkle with red pepper threads.

■ Ingredients (2 servings)

2 fillets (7oz／200g)　　mackerel

⅙ tsp　　salt

pinch of pepper

⅓oz／10g　　garlic, grated

2 sprigs　　thyme, minced

1　　zucchini

¼ lemon, cut into wedges

2 Tbs　　olive oil

❶ Make 2-3 slashes on the fish skin, sprinkle with salt and pepper and let stand for 10 minutes. Cut the zucchini into thin slices. Pour 1 Tbs of olive oil over them, then bake in a toaster oven.

❷ Blend the garlic and the thyme.

❸ Wipe the moisture off the fish. Sprinkle ② over the skin side and then pour 1 Tbs of olive oil.

Grilled Mackerel with Herbs

20min.
464kcal

A toaster oven is very handy for grilling fish and gives a nice finish.

❹ Bake in a toaster oven (or on a grill) until cooked through and lightly browned. Serve with lemon wedge.

Menu:　Tomato Salad／Julienne Vegetables Soup／Toasted Bread with Garlic

Menu: Mild Pumpkin Salad (p.49)／Quick Simmered Chinese Cabbage (p.58)／Clear Soup／Steamed Rice

13min.
206kcal

Sautéed Scallop with Butter-Soy Sauce

The flavor of the sautéed scallop is enhanced by the butter-soy mixture. The texture is crisp on the outside, yet rare on the inside.

■ Ingredients (2 servings)

6 (7oz／200g)

     scallops, edible raw

pinch of salt and pepper

1 Tbs   flour

4   green asparagus

2 Tbs   butter

1 Tbs   white wine

1 tsp   soy sauce

❶ Cut the asparagus and boil to desired tenderness.

❷ Properly prepare the scallops (see picture). Sprinkle with salt and pepper, then dust with flour.

❸ Melt 1 Tbs of butter in a skillet and begin to pan-broil the scored side. When lightly browned, turn over, pan-broil very briefly and remove.

❹ Add 1 Tbs of butter to the same skillet and make a sauce,

blending the wine and soy sauce with butter. Pour over the scallops.

Score one side of the scallop in a square pattern with sides of ³⁄₁₆ inch ／5mm. This gives the scallop an attractive finish and also allows the flavor to absorb well.

■ Ingredients (2 servings)

6   scallops, edible raw

A ⎡ pinch of salt and pepper
  ⎣ ½ Tbs   sake

3   eggs

B ⎡ 1 Tbs   milk
  ⎣ pinch of salt and pepper

2 Tbs   vegetable oil

pinch of sesame oil

❶ Cut the scallops in half crosswise and season with A.

❷ Beat the eggs and add B. Heat the vegetable oil in a skillet. Slip the beaten eggs into the skillet. Make loose scrambled eggs by mixing roughly and remove to a plate.

❸ Add the sesame oil to the

Menu: Grilled Vegetables with Olive Oil (p.65)／Spinach Soup／Bread

Scallop with Scrambled Eggs

15min.
363kcal

same skillet and briefly pan-broil the scallops on both sides.

❹ Add the scrambled eggs back to the skillet and roughly mix with the scallops. Remove and serve.

Baked Oysters

18min.
114kcal

This is a "one-pot" style dish of miso-flavored oysters. Using aluminum foil instead of a pot makes this recipe quicker and easier.

■ Ingredients (2 servings)

7oz／200g   shucked oysters

½   negi (long onion)

3½oz／100g   shirataki (p.96)

A ⎡ 1½ Tbs   miso
  ⎜ ½ Tbs   sugar
  ⎜ 1 Tbs   sake
  ⎣ ½ tsp   soy sauce

❶ Wash the oysters well in salt water(1 tsp salt per cup of water), and drain in a colander.

❷ Cut the long onion diagonally. Briefly blanch the shirataki and cut into 2inch／5cm lengths.

❸ Combine A.

❹ Lay out 2 aluminum foil squares. Place the shirataki, long onion and oysters on each foil square and pour A over everything. Fold the edge of the foil and seal firmly so as not to spill the juice. Bake in a toaster oven for about 10 minutes.

Menu: Steamed Tofu Chinese Style(p.69)／Soup／Steamed Rice

Sautéed Squid and Chingensai

15 min.
259 kcal

Proper preparation of the squid, while a little troublesome, gives a full-flavored finish to this simple recipe.

Cut the hood into 1½inch／4cm widths. Make ³⁄₁₆-inch／5-mm-wide diagonal slashes one way, then the other(do not cut all the way through the flesh) (left) and cut into 1⅙inch／3cm lengths(right).

■ Ingredients (2 servings)

7oz／200g　　rolled squid

A
　¼ tsp　　　salt
　1 Tbs　　　sake
　½ tsp　　　ginger juice
　1 Tbs　　　cornstarch

12⅔oz／360g

　chingensai(bok choy with green stems)

B
　½ tsp　　　bouillon powder
　100cc　　　water
　1 Tbs　　　sake
　⅓ tsp　　　salt
　2 tsp　　　cornstarch

2 Tbs　　　vegetable oil

❶ Separate the chingensai into stalks and leaves and cut into approx.2inch／5cm lengths. Combine B.

❷ Cut the squid (see picture) and season with A. Blanch in boiling water and remove as soon as heated through. Drain in a colander.

❸ Heat the oil in a skillet. Sauté first the stalks of chingensai, then the leaves, and add the squid. Pour B and mix well to coat everything. When it begins to bubble, remove from heat and serve.

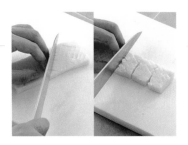

Menu: Grilled Vegetables with Olive Oil(p.65)／Soup／Bread

Rosemary Squid

15 min.
337 kcal

This is a good way to use fresh squid in season. Smaller squids produce a more tender finish.

■ Ingredients (2 servings)

2 (18oz／500g) squids
2 dried red peppers
⅔oz／20g garlic
3 Tbs olive oil
2 to 3 sprigs rosemary
A ⌈ 1 Tbs white wine
  │ ¼ tsp salt
  └ pinch of pepper

❶ To clean the squid, pull the hood away from the tentacles and remove the entrails from the hood. Cut off the tentacles just below the eyes, discarding the head. Cut the hood into rings and the tentacles and tail into manageable sizes. Seed the red peppers. Thinly slice the garlic.

❷ Heat the oil in a skillet. Sauté the garlic and red pepper over low heat. When the garlic turns light brown, add the squid and rosemary and sauté over high heat.

❸ When the squid are opaque, add A and stir, making sure the squid are completely coated.

Curried Squid

15 min.
178 kcal

■ Ingredients (2 servings)

1 (10½oz／300g) squid
½ onion
1 bel pepper
3½oz／100g shimeji mushrooms
⅓oz／10g garlic, thinly sliced
1 Tbs white wine
A ⌈ 1 tsp bouillon powder
  └ ½ tsp curry powder
1 Tbs vegetable oil

❶ Remove the tentacles and entrails from the hood. Cut the hood into approx.1⅛inch／3cm rectangles and the tentacles and tail into manageable sizes.

❷ Cut the onion into approx.½-inch／1½-cm-wide wedges and the bell pepper into ⅜-inch／1-cm-wide pieces. Separate the shimeji into small bunches.

❸ Heat ½ Tbs of oil in a skillet. Sauté the garlic over low heat until aromatic. Turn up the heat and sauté the squid until opaque. Add the wine. Cover and simmer for 1 to 2 minutes.

❹ Add ½ Tbs of oil, then add the vegetables and sauté over high heat. When the vegetables are done, add A and stir to coat.

Menu: Harusame Salad／Clam and Watercress Soup(p.83)／Steamed Rice

Sautéed Komatsuna and Harusame

15 min.
149 kcal

■ Ingredients (2 servings)

7oz／200g
   komatsuna (greens)

1oz／30g   harusame(bean thread)

2inch／5cm   negi (long onion)

2   dried shiitake mushrooms

A ⎡ 1 Tbs   oyster sauce
   | 1 tsp   soy sauce
   ⎣ 50cc   shiitake-soaking water

1 Tbs   sesame oil

❶ Soak the shiitakes in about 60cc water until soft and large, then cut into ³⁄₁₆inch／5mm squares. Cut the komatsuna into 2 inch／5cm lengths. Coarsely mince the long onion. Using kitchen scissors, cut the bean thread into 2inch／5cm lengths without soaking in water.

❷ Combine A.

❸ Heat the oil in a skillet. Sauté the long onion and shiitakes. When the flavor is released, add the komatsuna and sauté until the leaves are wilted. Add A and the bean thread and sauté until all the liquid is gone.

Chingensai with Mustard Dressing

10 min.
172 kcal

Any leafy greens go well with this recipe. Nigauri (bitter melon) is a good substitute as well.

■ Ingredients (2 servings)

7oz／200g   chingensai(bok choy with green stems)

1 small can (3oz／85g)   flaked tuna

A ⎡ 1 Tbs   stone-ground mustard
   ⎣ ½ Tbs   mayonnaise

❶ Blanch the chingensai and cut into approx. 1⅙ inch／3cm lengths.

❷ Extract the excess oil from the canned tuna flakes and combine with A.

❸ Mix ① and ②.

Taipei Style Green Salad

7 min.
133 kcal

■ Ingredients(2 servings)

7oz／200g   leafy greens
   (e.g. spinach, komatsuna, bok choy)

½oz／13g   garlic

2 Tbs   vegetable oil

1 Tbs   soy sauce

1 tsp   roasted white sesame seeds

❶ Cut away the root clusters of the greens and cut into 2inch／5cm lengths. Mince the garlic.

❷ Blanch the greens. Drain in a colander without squeezing and transfer to a bowl.

❸ Put the oil in a small pan and sauté the garlic until aromatic, taking care not to scorch it. Remove and pour it over the greens. Add the soy sauce and sesame seeds and mix well.

Simmered Yam and Kelp

18 min.
102 kcal

Preparation for this recipe takes only 3 minutes! Afterwards just set over heat and simmer. It is not necessary to use dashi stock, as the kelp produces a delicious flavor. Potato or daikon radish can be used instead of yam.

■ Ingredients (2 servings)

7oz／200g	nagaimo(Chinese yam)
3½oz／100g	carrot
⅓oz／10g	kelp, fine slivers
300cc	water
1 Tbs	sugar
2 Tbs	sake
½ Tbs	soy sauce
1 tsp	rice vinegar

❶ Peel the yam and cut into ⅜-inch／1-cm-thick rounds. Cut the carrot into slightly thinner rounds than the yam.

❷ Put all the ingredients into a sauce pan, cover with a drop-lid and simmer for 10 to 15 minutes until the yam has softened.

Cheese-Topped Grilled Yam and Okra

10 min.
236 kcal

This is a really quick recipe, as it uses the yam and okra without blanching. A convenient dish for breakfast on a busy morning.

■ Ingredients (2 servings)

3½oz／100g	nagaimo(Chinese yam)
6	okras
2oz／60g	pizza cheese
2 to 4 Tbs	mayonnaise
pinch of soy sauce	

❶ Peel the yam and cut into ⅜inch／1cm cubes. Cut the okra into ⅜-inch／1-cm-wide rings.

❷ Place the yam and okra on a heat-proof plate, sprinkle with cheese and top with mayonnaise, drawing a circle on the vegetables and cheese. Bake in a toaster oven for about 5 minutes.

❸ Serve with a pinch of soy sauce, if preferred.

■ Ingredients (2 servings)

2	potatoes
½	onion
1 tsp	vegetable oil
1 Tbs	sake
½ tsp	bouillon powder
½ Tbs	soy sauce
⅒oz／3g	dried bonito flakes (p.96)
¼ sheet	yaki-nori (p.96)

❶ Cut the potato into approx. ⅜ inch／1cm sticks. Wrap and heat in a microwave oven for about 2 minutes. Cut the onion into ⅜-inch／1-cm-wide wedges.

❷ Heat the oil in a skillet and sauté the onion. When the onion is coated with oil, add the potato and sauté further.

❸ Add the sake and bouillon powder and briefly sauté. At the end sprinkle soy sauce over everything.

❹ Transfer to a plate and top with the bonito flakes and yaki-nori, if available.

Sautéed Potato and Onion

10 min.
156 kcal

Taro Dumplings

15 min.
268 kcal

In this recipe, frozen taros are just as delicious as fresh ones.

■ Ingredients (2 servings)

12		frozen taros
A	2 Tbs	miso
	1 Tbs	sugar
	½ Tbs	mirin
	3 Tbs	dashi stock

pinch of yuzu citron rind (p.96)

4   bamboo skewers

❶ Boil the taros whole without thawing until tender.

❷ Combine A in a pan. Place over moderate heat. Heat through by mixing with a spatula. Remove.

❸ When it has cooled a bit, add the grated yuzu citron rind.

❹ Place 3 taros on each skewer, and brush with the yuzu-miso paste.

Pumpkin and Sweet Potato Salad

10 min.
243 kcal

Using either pumpkin or sweet potato is also OK. Coffee cream can be substituted for heavy cream.

■ Ingredients (2 servings)
7oz／200g   pumpkin
3½oz／100g   sweet potato
A ┌ 50cc   milk and heavy cream
  │ 1 to 1½ tsp   curry powder
  │ ⅙ tsp   salt
  └ pinch of pepper

❶ Cut the pumpkin and the sweet potato into ½inch／1½cm cubes. Soak the sweet potato in water and drain in a colander.
❷ Arrange both on a plate, wrap and heat in a microwave oven for about 5 minutes until a bamboo skewer can be inserted smoothly.
❸ Combine A in a pan and simmer for 1 to 2 minutes until it thickens a little. Add ②, mix to coat and remove.

Pumpkin with Chinese Flavored Dressing

10 min.
123 kcal

Busy schedules often result in a lack of green and yellow vegetables in your meals. This recipe is a simple way to balance your diet.

■ Ingredients (2 servings)
7oz／200g   pumpkin
A ┌ 2 Tbs   rice vinegar
  │ 1 tsp   sugar and soy sauce
  │ pinch of salt
  └ 1 Tbs   sesame oil
½ Tbs   roasted white sesame seeds

❶ Cut the pumpkin into approx. ⅛-inch／3-mm-thick slices. Boil until slightly tender, taking care not to overcook.
❷ Combine A and dress the pumpkin. Add the sesame seeds and mix.

■ Ingredients(2 servings)

7oz／200g	frozen pumpkin	
⅔oz／20g	onion	
1⅖oz／40g	canned corn kernels	
pinch of salt and pepper		

A
- ½ egg
- 100cc heavy cream
- 50cc milk
- pinch of salt and pepper

2oz／60g   pizza cheese

❶ Thinly slice the onion.

❷ Place the frozen pumpkin and onion on a plate, uncovered, and heat in a microwave oven for about 2 minutes. Cut the pumpkin into ⅜-inch／1-cm-thick pieces.

❸ Place the pumpkin, onion and corn kernels on a heatproof

Quiche Style Pumpkin

15 min.
464 kcal

plate and sprinkle with salt and pepper. Combine A and mix well. Pour A onto the plate and lay the cheese on top. Bake in a toaster oven for 7 to 8 minutes until brown.

■ Ingredients (2 servings)

7oz／200g	pumpkin
½	cucumber
½	celery stalk

A
- 1½ Tbs rice vinegar
- 1½ Tbs vegetable oil
- less than 1 tsp sugar
- pinch of salt and pepper

❶ Cut the cucumber into thin rings and the celery into thin diagonal slices. Sprinkle a pinch of salt (optional) over both. When wilted, gently squeeze out the water.

❷ Cut the pumpkin into ½ inch／1½cm cubes. Wrap and heat in a microwave oven for about 3 minutes until a bamboo skewer can be inserted smoothly.

Mild Pumpkin Salad

12 min.
141 kcal

This dressing gives the salad a mild taste. A great recipe for those who don't care for sweet pumpkin.

❸ Combine A in a bowl and mix well. Soak the pumpkin in the dressing while hot, then add the cucumber and celery.

Mushrooms with Daikon

5 min.
41 kcal

Easy to cook and low in calories, this recipe requires just a brief simmer with ponzu-joyu(lemon-soy mixture). You can make it again and again!

■ Ingredients (2 servings)

3½oz／100g enoki mushrooms

6 shiitake mushrooms

1¾oz／50g nameko mushrooms

A ⎡ 3 Tbs ponzu-joyu (lemon-soy mixture)
⎣ 1 Tbs sake

5¼oz／150g daikon radish

❶ Cut away the root cluster of the enoki and cut in half. Thinly slice the shiitakes. Briefly wash the namekos to remove the sticky coating.

❷ Place all the mushrooms and A in a sauce pan and simmer for 1 to 2 minutes until tender.

❸ Grate the daikon, lightly squeeze out the water and place a sizeable amount on the mushrooms.

Eringi and Mitsuba Salad with Nori

10 min.
32 kcal

Grilling is the best way to enjoy the crisp texture of the eringi, but you can also blanch them. Thick shiitake mushrooms can be used as a delicious substitute for eringi.

Note: Ponzu-joyu (lemon-soy mixture) can be used instead of A.

■ Ingredients (2 servings)

3½oz／100g eringi mushrooms

1¾oz／50g mitsuba (p.96)

½ sheet yaki-nori (p.96)

A ⎡ 1 Tbs rice vinegar
⎢ 1 Tbs dashi stock
⎢ ½ Tbs soy sauce
⎣ ½ tsp sugar

❶ Grill the eringi until lightly browned. Tear into thin pieces lengthwise, then cut into approx.1⅙inch／3cm lengths.

❷ Pour boiling water over the mitsuba, rinse in cold water and drain. Cut into approx.1⅙inch／3cm lengths.

❸ Combine A in a bowl and dress with ① and ②. Crumple up the yaki-nori into pieces and mix with the rest.

■ Ingredients (2 servings)

a total of 10½oz／300g
   shimeji mushrooms, cap mushrooms,shiitake mushrooms, etc.
1¾oz／50g
   string beans(if available)
⅔oz／20g   garlic
2 Tbs   olive oil
½ tsp   bouillon powder
pinch of salt and pepper

❶ Divide the shimeji into small clusters. Cut the cap mushrooms and shiitakes into ¾-inch／5-mm-thick slices. Cut the string beans into manageable sizes. Slice each clove of garlic into about three pieces.

❷ Heat the oil in a skillet. Sauté the garlic over low heat until aromatic. Add all the mushrooms

Steamed Mushrooms with Garlic

10 min.
174 kcal

and string beans and sauté over high heat. Reduce the heat, cover and braise for 6 to 7minutes. Stir with a spatula 1 to 2 times

halfway through cooking.

❸ Add the bouillon powder, stirring once. Season with salt and pepper to taste.

■ Ingredients (2 servings)

3½oz／100g   shimeji mushrooms
3½oz／100g   enoki mushrooms

A ┌1 Tbs   rice vinegar
  │½ Tbs   soy sauce
  │½ tsp   sugar
  └½   small dried red pepper

❶ Separate the shimeji into small pieces. Cut away the root cluster of the enoki and cut in half.

❷ Seed the red pepper and chop into fine rings. Combine A.

❸ Briefly blanch both mushrooms in boiling water, drain and immediately soak in A.

Liàng Pán Style Mushroom Salad

10 min.
22 kcal

The pungent flavor of red pepper enhances the appetite. For best results, soak the mushrooms for about 20 minutes in the seasonings.

Ingredients (2 servings)

7oz/200g	cabbage
⅓oz/10g	garlic
1 Tbs	vegetable oil
A ⎡½ Tbs	oyster sauce
⎣½ Tbs	soy sauce

❶ Tear the cabbage into manageable pieces. Thinly slice the garlic.
❷ Heat the oil in a skillet and sauté the garlic over low heat. When it begins to smell, turn the heat up to high and sauté the cabbage.
❸ When everything is coated with oil, drizzle A over the cabbage.

Sautéed Cabbage with Oyster Sauce

8 min.
101 kcal

This recipe is simple, but its savory taste can be used often. It only requires a brief sauté over high heat.

Cabbage Stalks with Sesame Dressing

10 min.
56 kcal

Cabbage stalks are not typically used, but they produce a crisp texture in this recipe. Pickled wasabi (p.96) can be used instead of sesame paste.

Ingredients (2 servings)

1¾oz/50g	stalk parts of cabbage
½	cucumber
	pinch of salt
A ⎡1 Tbs	sesame paste
⎢1 tsp	soy sauce
⎣2 Tbs	dashi stock

❶ Cut the cabbage stalks into thin slices. Cut the cucumber in half lengthwise, then cut diagonally into thin slices. Sprinkle salt over both of them. When tender, squeeze out the water.
❷ Combine the ingredients for A and mix well with ①.

■ Ingredients (2 servings)
7oz／200g   cabbage
  1 Tbs   butter
  1 Tbs   flour
4   vienna sausages
A ⌈1 tsp   bouillon powder
  ⌊100cc   milk and water
2 Tbs   heavy cream
B [pinch each of nutmeg, salt and pepper]

❶ Cut the cabbage into large pieces. Make several diagonal slashes on the sausages.
❷ Melt the butter in a sauce pan and sauté the cabbage. When it is completely coated with the butter, sprinkle with flour and sauté for about 1 minute.
❸ Add A and the sausage and

Simmered Cabbage in Heavy Cream

20 min.
276 kcal

Enjoy the sweet, mild taste of cabbage coated with a soft cream sauce.

simmer for about 15 minutes. When the cabbage is tender, add the heavy cream. Adjust the seasoning with B.

■ Ingredients (2 servings)
7oz／200g   cabbage
⅓ tsp   salt
3½oz／100g
    canned whole kernels
¼   onion
A ⌈3 Tbs   French dressing
  ⌊1 Tbs   mayonnaise

❶ Cut the cabbage into thin strips. Sprinkle with salt, toss lightly and set aside for 5 minutes, then squeeze out the water.
❷ If the corn is frozen, thaw in boiling water. Slice the onion into thin pieces, rinse in water and squeeze.
❸ Combine A and dress ① and ②.

Cabbage and Corn Salad

This salad goes well as a side dish for curry or stew. The mixed flavor of French dressing and mayonnaise appeals to everyone.

12 min.
251 kcal

Simmered Daikon and Tofu Puff

20 min.
130 kcal

Using shaved bonito flakes (p.96) saves time in making the dashi stock, but still brings out a full-flavored finish. Halfway through, invert once, so that the flavor steeps well.

■ Ingredients (2 servings)

7oz／200g   daikon radish

2 pieces   abura-age(p.96)

A
   300cc   water
   ⅕oz／6g   dried bonito flakes
   ½ Tbs   sugar
   1 Tbs   sake

B
   1 Tbs   soy sauce
   pinch of salt

❶ Cut the daikon into ³⁄₁₆-inch／5-mm-thick rounds. Cut the abura-age into 4 to 6 pieces.

❷ Place A, the daikon and the abura-age in a pan and bring to a boil. When boiled, cover and simmer for about 5 minutes.

❸ Add B and continue simmering until the daikon is tender.

Daikon with Umeboshi

4 min.
18 kcal

Many people shy away from pickled Japanese plums because of their extreme sourness. However, they can work very well as a seasoning, which is what this recipe calls for.

■ Ingredients (2 servings)

5¼oz／150g   daikon radish

1   umeboshi (p.96), large size with tender pulp

❶ Cut the daikon into thin strips and put in a bowl.

❷ Seed the umeboshi and mix with the daikon, tearing it into small pieces by hand.

■ Ingredients (2 servings)

7oz／200g   daikon radish

10   perilla leaves (p.96)

A
- 1 Tbs
  each soy sauce, rice vinegar and vegetable oil
- 1 tsp   sugar
- 2 Tbs
  grated white sesame seeds

❶ Cut the daikon into approx.⅓-inch／2-mm-thick rectangles.

❷ Cut the perilla leaves into thin strips, then let soak in water and drain.

❸ Combine A and toss with the daikon and perilla leaves.

Daikon Salad with Sesame Dressing

This unique dressing has a flavorful taste.

5 min.
132 kcal

Sautéed Daikon and Littleneck Clams

■ Ingredients (2 servings)

10½oz／300g   daikon radish

3½oz／100g
   shucked littleneck clams

5 to 6   scallions

⅙oz／5g   ginger

1 Tbs   vegetable oil

A
- 1 Tbs   sake
- ⅙ tsp   salt
- 1 tsp   soy sauce

❶ Cut the daikon into approx.⅓-inch／2-mm-thick rectangles. Cut the scallion into 2inch／5cm lengths. Thinly slice the ginger. Wash the littleneck clams in cold water and drain.

❷ Combine the ingredients for A.

❸ Heat the oil in a skillet and sauté the ginger. When it begins to smell good, sauté the daikon and littleneck clams until they are coated with oil. Add A and sauté further until the daikon is tender.

❹ Add the scallion and remove from heat.

15 min.
125 kcal

Quick Eggplant

10 min.
40 Kcal

This dish can dress up an otherwise dull menu. Heating the dried bonito flakes in a microwave oven for 1 minute makes them more fragrant.

■ Ingredients (2 servings)

4	eggplants
1 bud	myoga ginger (p.96)
2 Tbs	ponzu-joyu(lemon-soy mixture)
approx.⅒oz／3g	dried bonito flakes (p.96)

❶ Cut the eggplant in half lengthwise, then slice thinly. Chop the myoga into thin rings.

❷ Soak the eggplants in water and drain. Without drying them, wrap and heat in a microwave oven for about 6 minutes, turning over once halfway through.

❸ Toss the eggplants and myoga together and coat with ponzu-joyu. Transfer to a serving dish and top with the bonito flakes.

Eggplant and Bell Pepper with Sesame Dressing

10 min.
56 kcal

The full-bodied eggplants flavored with sesame-vinegar dressing are delicious. This goes well as a side dish with Japanese, Chinese or Western cuisine.

■ Ingredients (2 servings)

2	eggplants
¼	large red bell pepper

A
- 2 tsp   each grated white sesame seeds, miso, rice vinegar, and soy sauce
- 1 tsp   sugar and vegetable oil

❶ Cut the eggplant into ³⁄₁₆-inch／5-mm-thick rounds and soak in water. Cut the bell pepper into ³⁄₁₆-inch／5-mm-wide x 1½-inch／4-cm-long pieces

❷ Blanch the eggplants in sufficient boiling water until tender, then drain in a colander. Boil the bell pepper in the same boiling water and drain.

❸ Combine A and mix with ②.

■ Ingredients (2 servings)

3   eggplants

2   pre-sliced chicken breast

   ½ Tbs   sake

   pinch of salt

4inch／10cm   negi (long onion)

A ⎡ 1 Tbs   sugar
   ⎢ 2 Tbs   rice vinegar
   ⎢ 1½ Tbs   soy sauce
   ⎢ ½ Tbs   sesame oil
   ⎢ 2inch／5cm   negi (long onion), minced
   ⎢ pinch of dried red pepper,
   ⎣   chopped into thin rings

❶ Cut the eggplant in half lengthwise. Wrap and heat in a microwave oven for 6 minutes.

❷ Remove the tendon from the chicken and sprinkle with sake and salt. Wrap and heat in a micro-

Steamed Eggplant and Chicken

15 min.
108 kcal

wave oven for 1½ to 2 minutes. Tear into thin strips while hot. Cut the long onion into threads and let soak in water.

❸ Thinly slice the eggplants. Arrange them with the chicken on a plate. Combine A and serve as a dip.

■ Ingredients (2 servings)

3   eggplants

4inch／10cm   negi (long onion)

2 Tbs   vegetable oil

2 Tbs   tián man qiang
       (Chinese sweet miso paste)

½ Tbs   sake and soy sauce

❶ Cut the eggplant in half lengthwise and into ⅜-inch／1-cm-thick diagonal pieces. Coarsely mince the long onion.

❷ Heat the oil in a skillet and sauté the eggplant until tender. Add the long onion and the tián man qiang separately and sauté briefly. Finally, add the sake and soy sauce and stir until the eggplant is well-coated.

Sautéed Eggplant with Chinese Sweet Miso

6 min.
177 kcal

Chinese sweet miso has a richer taste than Japanese miso. This savory dish goes well with hot steamed rice.

Quick Simmered Chinese Cabbage

8 min.
55 kcal

Cooking in a microwave oven softens the Chinese cabbage and reduces its bulk, making it possible to eat in large quantities at a time.

■ Ingredients (2 servings)
3 leaves (10½oz／300g)
  Chinese cabbage
1/10oz／3g   dried bonito flakes (p.96)

A ⌈ 1 Tbs   mirin
   | 1 Tbs   soy sause
   | ⅙ tsp   salt
   ⌊ 1 tsp   vegetable oil

❶ Separate the cabbage into leaves and stalks. Coarsely cut the leaves and the stalks into 2-inch／5-cm-long thin strips. Wrap and heat in a microwave oven for about 6 minutes, turning over halfway through.

❷ Combine A and toss lightly with ①.

❸ Transfer to a plate and lay the bonito flakes on top.

Butter-Sautéed Chinese Cabbage

5 min.
122 kcal

The sweet taste and crisp texture of Chinese cabbage is the key to this recipe. It is also suitable as a garnish.

■ Ingredients (2 servings)
3 leaves (10½oz／300g)
  Chinese cabbage
2 Tbs   butter
⅙ tsp   salt
pinch of pepper
½ tsp   soy sauce

❶ Divide the Chinese cabbage into leaves and stalks. Coarsely cut the leaves and the stalks into approx. ½inch/1½cm x 2inch /5cm rectangles.

❷ Sauté the stalks in butter over high heat until slightly tender. Add the leaves and sauté briefly. Reduce the heat, cover and braise for 1 to 2 minutes.

❸ Finally, adjust the seasoning with salt, pepper and soy sauce.

■ Ingredients (2 servings)

2 leaves (7oz／200g)
　Chinese cabbage
½　　apple
1½inch／4cm　　celery stalk
⅔oz／20g　　raisins
A ⌈ 4 Tbs　　plain yoghurt
　│ 1 Tbs　　mayonnaise
　└pinch each of stone ground mustard, salt and pepper

❶ Divide the Chinese cabbage into leaves and stalks. Coarsely cut the leaves and the stalks into thin strips. Cut the celery into pieces about the same size as the cabbage stalk.

❷ Cut the apple into ⅛-inch／3-mm-thick quarter-rounds. Soak the raisins in lukewarm water until plump, then drain.

15 min.
119 kcal

Chinese Cabbage and Apple Salad

The secret of this recipe is in the combination of the tender leaves and crisp stalks of Chinese cabbage. The fresh Chinese cabbage also makes a delicious ingredient.

❸ Put a pinch of salt(optional) in cold water and let the cabbage, apple and celery soak until crisp, then drain.

❹ Combine A and toss with ③ and the raisins.

■ Ingredients (2 servings)

3 leaves (10½oz／300g)
　Chinese cabbage
1 can (6³⁄₁₀oz／180g)　　salmon
100cc　　canned white sauce
approx.100cc　　milk
1¾oz／50g
　cheese, a kind that melts well
pinch of salt and pepper

❶ Coarsely cut the cabbage, wrap and heat in a microwave oven for about 6 minutes, turning over halfway through.Drain and sprinkle with salt and pepper.

❷ Blend the milk into the white sauce little by little. Season with salt and pepper to taste.

❸ Spread half of the white sauce on a heatproof plate and place

Chinese Cabbage and Salmon au Gratin

20 min.
382 kcal

the cabbage on it. Drain the liquid from the canned salmon and flake into pieces. Spread them over the cabbage and drizzle

with the remaining white sauce. Sprinkle with cheese.

❹ Bake in a toaster oven for 7 to 8 minutes until brown.

Quick Simmered Lettuce and Prawns

15 min.
66 kcal

The key to this recipe is not to heat the lettuce too much. Remove it from the heat while it is crisp.

■ Ingredients (2 servings)

½ (7oz／200g)		lettuce
4		prawns
	½ tsp	sake and cornstarch
⅙oz／5g		ginger
A	200cc	dashi stock
	1 Tbs	mirin
	⅓ tsp	salt
	½ tsp	soy sauce

❶ Cut the lettuce into 4 portions and the ginger into julienne strips.

❷ Shell and devein the prawns. Cut into 3 portions and dust with sake and cornstarch.

❸ Put A in a pan and bring to a boil. Add the prawns and ginger and cook briefly. Add the lettuce and heat until it is slightly wilted. Remove and serve.

Lettuce and Scallop Salad

5 min.
122 kcal

Scallop flakes work fine for this recipe. This saves the time needed to flake the scallops into pieces, as well as being a cheaper option. The combination of daikon radish and scallop is well-known, but scallop also goes very well with lettuce.

■ Ingredients (2 servings)

½ (5¼oz／150g)		lettuce
1 small can (approx.1¾oz／50g)		scallop flakes
5		scallions
A	1 Tbs	soy sauce
	1 Tbs	rice vinegar
	1 Tbs	vegetable oil
	1½ Tbs	canned scallop juice

❶ Cut the lettuce into the thicker strips.

❷ Cut the scallions into 1⅛ inch／3cm lengths.

❸ Combine A.

❹ Lightly toss the lettuce, scallion and scallop flakes together and pour A over them.

■ Ingredients (2 servings)

7oz／200g lettuce

3½oz／100g shimeji mushrooms

1 Tbs vegetable oil

A ⎡1 Tbs salted kombu kelp, thinly sliced
⎣2 Tbs ponzu-joyu(lemon-soy mixture)

❶ Cut the lettuce into manageable pieces. Separate the shimeji into small clusters.

❷ Heat the oil in a skillet, sauté the shimejis until tender and add the lettuce. Just before the lettuce has cooked down, add A and mix lightly. Remove and serve.

Sautéed Lettuce with Salted Kelp

Salted kombu kelp is a very useful seasoning.

5 min.
93 kcal

Bell Pepper Salad with Salted Kombu Kelp

Cut the bell pepper into thin strips and blanch briefly. Mix with the salted kombu kelp threads while they are hot.

■ Ingredients (2 servings)

10½oz／300g lettuce

2 rashers bacon

⅙oz／5g garlic

½ Tbs olive oil

pinch of salt and pepper

❶ Cut the lettuce into manageable sizes.

❷ Cut the bacon into ⅜-inch／1-cm-wide pieces. Thinly slice the garlic.

❸ Heat the oil in a skillet and sauté the garlic and bacon over low heat.

❹ Turn the heat up. Add the lettuce, sauté briefly and adjust the seasoning with salt and pepper.

Sautéed Lettuce with Bacon

When sautéed, the outer lettuce leaves make for an excellent dish.

8 min.
160 kcal

Asparagus Salad with Egg

12 min.
84 kcal

Egg yolk makes an interesting topping for asparagus. Boiled potatoes can be used instead of asparagus.

■ Ingredients (2 servings)
4 stalks   green asparagus
2   eggs
pinch of salt and pepper

❶ Peel the hard parts of the asparagus and cut in half.
❷ Put 1 tsp of salt (optional) in 3 cups of boiling water, boil the asparagus and drain in a colander.
❸ Poach the eggs in the same boiling water. Break the egg and drop it into boiling water. Continue to boil for 4 to 5 minutes, making the egg white a good shape using chopsticks.
❹ Arrange the asparagus on a plate and lay the egg on top. Sprinkle with salt and pepper.

Bean Sprouts with Chinese Chile Sauce

10 min.
74 kcal

■ Ingredients (2 servings)
7oz/200g
    bean sprouts or soybean sprouts
½   small red bell pepper

A
  1 Tbs   rice vinegar
  1 tsp   sugar and soy sauce
  ¼ tsp   tou ban qiang
         (Chinese chile sauce)
  ½ tsp   sesame oil
  pinch of salt

❶ Blanch the bean sprouts according to the package instructions. Drain in a colander and lightly squeeze out the water.
❷ Cut the bell pepper into pieces as thick as the bean sprouts and boil briefly.
❸ Combine the ingredients for A and mix with ① and ②.

■ Ingredients (2 servings)

1¾oz／50g　nira (p.96)

3½oz／100g　enoki mushrooms

A ┌ ½ Tbs　miso and mirin
　 └ ½ tsp　rice vinegar

½ tsp　vegetable oil

1 tsp　roasted white sesame seeds

❶ Cut the nira into 1⅛inch／3cm lengths. Cut off the root cluster of the enoki, cut in half crosswise and separate slightly.

❷ Combine the ingredients for A.

❸ Heat the oil in a skillet and briefly sauté the enoki, then the nira. Add A and stir with the enoki and nira to coat. Transfer to a plate and sprinkle with sesame seeds.

Nira and Enoki with Sesame-Miso Dressing

Nira, or Chinese leek, should be used more frequently, as it is one of the cheap ingredients available year-round. By adding miso, its strong smell can be removed, making it easier to eat.

5 min.
46 kcal

■ Ingredients (2 servings)

3½oz／100g　soybean sprouts

⅞oz／25g　mitsuba (p.96)

1oz／30g　carrot

1　abura-age (p.96)

1/2 Tbs　soy sauce

1/2 tsp　sesame oil

❶ Cut the mitsuba into 1⅛ inch／3cm lengths and the carrot into 1⅛-inch／3-cm-long julienne strips.

❷ Grill the abura-age in a toaster oven until golden brown. Cut in half lengthwise, then into ⅜-inch／1-cm-wide pieces.

❸ Put 2 cups of water and ¼ tsp of salt (optional) in a pan. Add the soybean sprouts and carrot,

Crisp Soybean Sprouts

10 min.
81 kcal

Putting the soybean sprouts in cold water and bringing them to a boil gives a crisp finish.

cover and bring to a boil. 1 minute after boiling, add the mitsuba and remove from heat immediately. Drain in a colander.

❹ While still hot, coat the vegetables with soy sauce and sesame oil. Right before serving, add ② and toss lightly.

Bean and Lotus Root Salad

Unseasoned canned beans are edible as they are, but heating them a little produces a softer, moister texture.

■ Ingredients (2 servings)

2⅘oz／80g   unseasoned canned large red beans

3½oz／100g   lotus root

3½oz／100g   string beans

A
- 2⅘oz／80g   cottage cheese
- 2 Tbs   milk
- 1 tsp   rice vinegar
- 1 tsp   onion, minced
- pinch of salt and pepper

❶ Cut the string beans and the lotus root into manageable pieces. Soak the lotus in water to remove the harsh taste.

❷ Briefly parboil ① in lightly salted water, then add the red beans and continue boiling for 1 to 2 minutes. Drain.

❸ Combine A and toss with ②.

Broccoli Topped with Chirimen-jako

Roasted chirimen-jako(p.96) goes well as a topping for a lettuce, boiled cabbage, daikon radish, tofu, etc..

■ Ingredients (2 servings)

7oz／200g   broccoli

1 tsp   soy sauce

⅓oz／10g   garlic

⅔oz／20g   chirimen-jako (p.96)

1 Tbs   vegetable oil

❶ Separate the broccoli into small florets. Blanch in lightly salted water, then sprinkle with soy sauce.

❷ Thinly slice the garlic.

❸ Heat the oil in a skillet and briefly sauté the garlic over low heat. Add the chirimen-jako and continue to sauté until everything is light brown. Remove.

❹ Transfer ① to a plate and sprinkle with ③.

Ingredients (2 servings)

1   zucchini

2   eggplants

½   large red bell pepper

2 Tbs   olive oil

pinch of salt and pepper

❶ Cut the zucchini into ³⁄₁₆-inch／5-mm-thick diagonal slices. Stem the eggplants and cut into ³⁄₁₆-inch／5-mm-thick pieces length-wise. Cut the bell pepper into manageable sizes.

❷ Grill the vegetables, arrange them on a plate and serve with olive oil, salt and pepper, as desired.

Grilled Vegetables with Olive Oil

You can use many vegetables of your choice for this recipe. Extra-virgin olive oil gives a full-bodied finish to the recipe.

10 min.
164 kcal

Creative Uses for Leftover Vegetables

An easy option is to use vegetable leftovers as soup ingredients. However, if several kinds of vegetables are left over, they can be used to make fantastic salads, as in the following recipes:

Boil vegetables such as cabbage, carrot, daikon radish, turnip, burdock, mushrooms, or string beans, etc. and make a warm vegetable salad.

Vegetables which are edible raw, such as lettuce, celery, carrot, cabbage, or cucumber can be chopped to make a fresh vegetable salad. Finely shredding vegetables can make a little go a long way.

Tofu Dish Varieties

Tofu with Nira-Sesame Oil

This is best served with beer, as the nira's strong smell matches beer very well.

■ Ingredients (2 servings)

1 block   tofu

1¾oz／50g   nira(Chinese leeks)

A ⌈ 1 Tbs   soy sauce

    ⌊ 1 Tbs   sesame oil

❶ Chop the nira into fine pieces, mix with A and set aside for at least 30 minutes.

❷ Cut the tofu in half lengthwise, lay ① on top and pour the liquid over and around the tofu.

Tofu Steak with Crab Meat and Cheese

■ Ingredients (2 servings)

1 block   "cotton" tofu

2   slices cheese

Approx.1⅛oz／35g   canned crab meat

1   scallion

❶ Cut the tofu in half crosswise, wrap in a paper towel and set aside to allow it to drain.

❷ Chop the scallion into fine pieces. Remove the cartilage from the crab meat and flake into pieces.

❸ Melt 1 Tbs of butter in a skillet. Dredge the tofu in 1 Tbs of flour and pan-broil on both sides.

❹ Lay ② on top of the tofu. Pour 1 Tbs of soy sauce over it, and place the cheese on top. Cover and heat until the cheese melts. Remove and serve.

Deep-Fried Tofu

■ Ingredients (2 servings)

1 block   "cotton" tofu

1 Tbs   flour

oil for deep-frying

1 Tbs   ginger, grated

A ⌈ ¼oz／2g

    | bonito flakes

    | 1½ Tbs   soy sauce and mirin

    ⌊ 50cc   water

❶ Cut the tofu into quarters, then remove the moisture using a paper towel. ❷ Bring A (combined) to a boil, then strain. ❸ Just before deep-frying, dredge the tofu in flour. Deep-fry it in 340°F／170°C oil. Transfer to a plate. ❹ Lay the ginger on top of the tofu and pour A over everything.

★**One block of tofu used in the recipes on p.66-67 weights 10½oz／300g.**

Tofu au Gratin

■ Ingredients (2 servings)

1 block	"cotton" tofu		3 Tbs	heavy cream
¼ tsp	salt		2 Tbs	mayonnaise
pinch of pepper		A	½ tsp	sugar
3½oz／100g	spinach		½ tsp	stone-ground mustard
½ Tbs	butter		⅓oz／10g	pizza cheese

❶ Wrap the tofu in a paper towel and remove as much liquid as possible. Roughly crush the tofu and sprinkle with salt and pepper.

❷ Briefly blanch the spinach until slightly wilted, cut into 1⅛inch/3cm lengths and firmly squeeze out the water. Sauté in the butter.

❸ Spread out the spinach on a heatproof dish and lay the tofu on top. Mix A and pour over the tofu and spinach. Sprinkle with cheese and bake in a toaster oven for 4 to 5 minutes.

■ Ingredients (2 servings)

½ block   "cotton" tofu

1¾oz／50g   pork ham, thinly sliced

3½oz／100g   soybean sprouts

1¾oz／50g   nira(Chinese leeks)

1½ Tbs   vegetable oil

A ⎡pinch of salt
  ⎣⅙oz／5g   bonito flakes

½ Tbs   soy sauce

❶ Cut the tofu in half crosswise and into ⅜-inch/1-cm-thick pieces. Blanch briefly in boiling water containing a sprinkle of salt.

❷ Cut the pork into 1⅛inch/3cm lengths and the nira into 2inch/5cm lengths.

❸ Heat 1 Tbs of oil in a skillet and pan-broil the tofu on both sides until lightly browned. Add A and stir, coating the tofu. Remove and set aside.

❹ Add ½ Tbs of oil to the skillet and sauté

Sautéed Tofu, Pork and Vegetables

This healthy dish is typical of Okinawan cuisine. Nigauri (bitter melon) is generally used there.

first the meat, then the soybean sprouts and finally the nira. Return the tofu to the pan and sprinkle with soy sauce. Turn off the heat at once.

Steamed Tofu; Chinese Style

This recipe is at once easy, delicious and economical. Only a serving bowl is necessary for this recipe, so it is very easy to make and quick to clean up.

15 min.
257 kcal

■ Ingredients (2 servings)

1 block (10½oz／300g) "silk" tofu (p.96)

1¾oz／50g ground pork

1⅖oz／40g bottled za cài (Chinese hot pickles)

A [1 Tbs each soy sauce, sake, sesame oil and cornstarch]

⅙oz／5g ginger

3 scallions

❶ Wrap the tofu in a paper towel and let drain until ready to use.

❷ Coarsely mince the za cài. Mince the ginger. Chop the scallion into fine rings.

❸ Put the meat, za cài, and A(combined) in the larger sized microwave-safe dish and mix. Add the crushed tofu and toss everything lightly. Wrap and heat in a microwave oven for about 6 min..

❹ Top with ginger and scallion to finish.

Tofu Steak Topped with Jako

12 min.
275 kcal

If a recipe requires you to heat tofu, a microwave oven can be used to drain it. Wrap the tofu in a paper towel, then heat for about 2 minutes per block(10½ oz/300 g).

■ Ingredients (2 servings)

1 block (10½oz／300g) "cotton" tofu (p.96)

3 Tbs (⅓oz／10g) chirimen-jako (p.96)

3 perilla leaves (p.96)

⅓oz／10g garlic

1 Tbs vegetable oil

A [1Tbs soy sauce and sake]

❶ Wrap the tofu in a paper towel and heat in a microwave oven for about 2 minutes to drain. Cut into 2 pieces lengthwise and cut each piece in half crosswise.

❷ Pour the hot water over the chirimen-jako. Thinly slice the perilla leaves and the garlic. Soak the perilla leaves in water and drain.

❸ Heat the oil in a skillet and sauté the garlic over low heat until lightly browned. Remove and set aside.

❹ Put the tofu in the skillet and pan-fry on both sides over high heat until golden brown. Sprinkle with A and evenly coat the tofu. Transfer to a plate and pile the chirimen-jako, perilla leaves and garlic on the tofu.

One-Pot Simmered Tofu

Bonito flakes are put in the pot directly instead of making a dashi stock. This is also good as a condiment to eat with tofu.

■ Ingredients (2 servings)

1 block(10½oz／300g)
    "silk" tofu (p.96)

⅙oz／5g   dried bonito flakes(p.96)

A ⎰ 2 Tbs   soy sauce
⎱ 1 Tbs   sugar and sake
    100cc   water

2   eggs

4 to 5   scallions (if available)

❶ Cut the tofu into 1⅛inch/3cm squares and the scallions into 1½ inch/4cm lengths.

❷ Lay the bonito flakes in the earthenware casserole and arrange the tofu on top. Add A, cover and set over moderate heat. When boiled, reduce the heat and simmer for about 5 minutes to absorb the flavor.

❸ Pour in the beaten eggs. When the eggs have cooked to desired firmness, sprinkle with scallions, if desired. Remove and carry to the table.

One more dish in an instant!

Place a piece of kombu kelp in a plate, top with ½ block tofu and sprinkle with a pinch of sake. Heat unwrapped in a microwave oven for about 2 minutes.

Ingredients (2 servings)

8 slices(approx.5¼oz／150g) pork, wafer-thin slices

1 block (6⅓oz／180g) atsu-age(p.96)

3½oz／100g enoki mushrooms

⅓oz／10g ginger

1 Tbs sake

A
┌ 1 Tbs sake
│ ½-odd Tbs soy sauce
│ 1 tsp bouillon powder and cornstarch
└ 50cc water

1 scallion, chopped into fine rings

❶ Cut off the root cluster of the enoki and cut in half. Cut the ginger into julienne strips. Pour boiling water over the atsu-age and cut into 8 pieces crosswise.

Rolled Pork

15 min.
412 kcal

This quick microwave dish has a surprisingly nice finish.

❷ Spread out the meat, place one portion of the atsu-age and the ginger on it and roll up.

❸ Arrange 8 rolls on a dish and sprinkle with sake. Wrap and heat in a microwave oven for about 4 minutes. Combine A.

❹ Discard the liquid drawn out from the pork rolls while heating. Sprinkle the rolls with the enokis, then pour A over everything. Wrap again and heat for about 2 minutes. Transfer to a plate and sprinkle with scallions, if desired.

Ingredients (2 servings)

2 pieces abura-age(p.96)

2 mochi (rice cake made by pounding steamed glutinous rice into a cake)

⅔oz／20g pickled nozawana (a variety of turnips)

1 Tbs neri-uni(seasoned sea urchin egg paste)

❶ Cut the abura-age in half and open them up into pouches. Pour boiling water over them to rinse off excess oil.

❷ Mince the nozawana coarsely.

❸ Cut the rice cakes in half and put one piece each into the 4 abura-age pouches. Put the nozawana in 2 of them and sea urchin in

Rice Cake in Tofu-Puff Pouches

10 min.
228 kcal

This light recipe makes an ideal side dish for a tea break.

the rest. Secure the open ends with toothpicks.

❹ Bake the pouches in a toaster oven for about 3 minutes, turn over and bake for another 3 minutes.

Ingredients (2 servings)

1 piece(7oz／200g)
white konnyaku jelly (p.96)

½ Tbs vegetable oil

A ┌ 1½ Tbs soy sauce
│ 2 Tbs mirin
└ 3 Tbs dashi stock or water

(for seasonings)

B ┌ ground black sesame seeds
│ bonito flakes (p.96)
└ 7-spice pepper (p.96)

8 min.
87 kcal

Kaminari Konnyaku

Kaminari means thunder. Kaminari Konnyaku is named for the large sizzling sound made when konnyaku is put in a heated pan. Several varieties can be made by changing the seasonings.

❶ Tear the konnyaku into bite-sized pieces using a spoon. Blanch briefly in boiling water.

❷ Heat the oil in a pan and sauté the konnyaku over high heat to let its moisture evaporate. When it turns whitish, add A and roast over high heat until all the liquid is gone.

❸ Separate the konnyaku into 3 portions and mix each portion with one of the seasonings in B.

Konnyaku and Nigauri in Vinegar-Miso Dressing

10 min.
59 kcal

The secret of this recipe is in the contrasting combination of the neutral flavor of konnyaku and the strong flavor of nigauri. Briefly boiled wakegi shallot or lettuce can be used instead of nigauri.

Ingredients (2 servings)

½ (3½oz／100g)
white konnyaku jelly (p.96)

½ (4⅕oz／120g) nigauri
(bitter melon)

A ┌ 1½ Tbs miso
│ 1 Tbs sugar and rice vinegar
└ ⅓ tsp karashi(Jap.mustard)

❶ Cut the konnyaku in half lengthwise, then cut each piece in half horizontally. Slice the four pieces into rectangles.

❷ Cut the nigauri in half lengthwise. Remove the seeds and fleecy part using a spoon, then cut into thin slices. Briefly blanch the nigauri and konnyaku one by one.

❸ Combine A and mix with ②.

Ingredients (2 servings)

7oz／200g   shirataki (p.96)

A ⎡ 1½ Tbs   soy sauce
  ⎣ 1 Tbs   mirin and sake

1   egg

   pinch of salt

  1 tsp   vegetable oil

1 to 2   scallions

⅒oz／3g   dried bonito flakes

❶Cut the shiratakis into 2inch /5cm lengths and blanch briefly. Cut the scallions into ⅜inch/5 mm lengths.

❷Beat the egg and add the salt. Heat the oil in a pan. Scramble the egg and remove from the pan.

❸Put the shirataki and A in the pan and stir until most of the liq-

Toasted Shirataki

Shirataki filaments stay fresh as long as konnyaku. It can be conveniently stocked in the refrigerator to use in other recipes.

uid is absorbed.Add the scallions and remove from heat.

❹Add the scrambled egg and the bonito flakes.

Ingredients (2 servings)

1 piece(7oz／200g)

   konnyaku jelly (p.96)

A ⎡ 1 Tbs   soy sauce and sake
  ⎢ 1 tsp   bouillon powder
  ⎣ 1 tsp   rice vinegar

3½oz／100g   canned corn kernels

1 Tbs   butter

½ Tbs   vegetable oil

❶ Cut the konnyaku in half. Make approx. ⅜-inch/5-mm-deep fine diagonal slashes on both sides, then make approx. ½-inch/1½-cm-wide deep cuts (see picture). Blanch in boiling water for 1 to 2 minutes.

❷ Combine A. Melt ½ Tbs of butter in a skillet. Sauté the corn

Konnyaku Steak in Butter

Scoring a few deep cuts in the konnyaku makes it easier to eat with chopsticks.

kernels and transfer to a plate.

❸ Add the vegetable oil to the skillet and pan-broil both sides of the konnyaku until well browned.

❹ Add A and ½ Tbs of butter, coat the konnyaku well and transfer to the plate.

This oil-free, versatile dressing is worth learning how to make,as it can be used in many ways.

❶ Soak the kiriboshi-daikon in boiling water for about 3 minutes.
❷ Cut the cucumber into the smaller wedges, rotating as you cut. Slice the tomato into rounds. Cut the lettuce into ⅜-inch/1-cm-wide strips.
❸ Firmly squeeze out the water from the daikon. Cut into manageable lengths and mix with ②.
❹ Transfer to a dish and sprinkle with sesame seeds. Combine A. Serve with A as a dressing.

8 min.
59 kcal

Kiriboshi-Daikon Salad

■ Ingredients (2 servings)

⅔oz／20g	kiriboshi-daikon (dried daikon radish threads)	1 large leaf	lettuce
½	cucumber	A [1 Tbs	each soy sauce, mirin and rice vinegar]
3	cherry tomatoes	1 tsp	roasted white sesame seeds

Kiriboshi-Daikon in Sweet Vinegar

10 min.
70 kcal

■ Ingredients (2 servings)

⅔oz／20g	kiriboshi-daikon (dried daikon radish threads)	⅓oz/10g	ginger
½	negi (long onion)	A ⎡1 Tbs	soy sauce
		1 Tbs	rice vinegar
		½ Tbs	sugar and sesame oil

Make in large batches and store as a reserve dish,or serve with beer.This dressing goes well with almost all the vegetables.

❶ Cut the long onion and the ginger into desired-size julienne strips.
❷ Briefly blanch the kiriboshi-daikon in boiling water.Squeeze out the water and cut into approx.1½inch/4cm lengths. Soak in A(combined), then add the long onion(set aside some for decoration) and the ginger. Mix everything together.
❸ Transfer to a dish and pile the reserved long onion on top.

■ Ingredients (2 servings)

⅙oz／5g	dried hijiki (P.96)
1 piece	abura-age (P.96)
2	eggs

A ⎡1 Tbs　　sugar and soy sauce
　⎣150cc　　water

❶ Lightly wash the hijiki and drain. Cut the abura-age in half and open into a pouch. Pour boiling water over the pouches.

❷ Make a stuffed pouch and secure the open end with a toothpick.

❸ Heat A to a boil. Add ②,cover and simmer over moderate heat for about 10 minutes until all the cooking liquid is absorbed.

❹ Cut the pouch in half.

15 min.
160 kcal

Quick Simmered Tofu-Puff Pouches

This dish is delicious served cold, so it is good for a box-lunch.

To make a stuffed tofu-puff pouch easily, place a tofu-puff pouch into a Japanese tea cup or similar item, and stuff first a raw egg, then hijiki into it.

■ Ingredients (2 servings)

½oz／15g	yaki-fu (baked fu)
1	cucumber
¼ tsp	salt
⅓oz／10g	ginger

A ⎡½ Tbs　　sugar
　⎢2 Tbs　　dashi stock
　⎢1½ Tbs　　rice vinegar
　⎣pinch of salt

❶ Soften the fu for 5 minutes in water, then squeeze out the water. Cut into manageable sizes.

❷ Cut the cucumber into thin rings. Sprinkle with salt and set aside for about 3 minutes. Squeeze. Cut the ginger into julienne strips.

❸ Combine A and dress ① and ② with it.

Fu and Cucumber Salad

This salad has a surprising mix of the opposing soft and crisp textures of fu and cucumber. The fu(a light cake made of wheat gluten) absorbs dressing well, so reduce the amount of salt you usually put in a dressing.

12 min.
45 kcal

One-Pot Cooking

One-pot cooking is very handy when you are busy. These great exampl

Milk Soup with Taro and Salmon

■ Ingredients (2 servings)
1 fillet (3½oz∕100g) fresh salmon
½ onion
12 frozen taros
2½oz/70g canned corn kernels
A ┌ 600cc water
  └ 3 Tbs sake
B ┌ 50cc milk
  └ 2 to 3 Tbs miso

❶ Sprinkle a pinch of salt(optional) over the fish and cut into bite-sized pieces. Par-boil briefly in boiling water and drain. Thinly slice the onion.
❷ Bring A to a boil. Add the taros and ① and skim off any scum and froth. Dissolve the miso in the milk (B). When the taros are tender, add B and the corn kernels.
❸ Serve with 7-spice pepper, if desired.

■ Ingredients (2 servings)
4 frankfurt sausages
2 potatoes
3½oz∕100g lettuce
½(approx.7oz/200g) unseasoned canned tomato and liquid
A [2 bouillon cubes, 600cc water]
B [pinch each of salt, pepper and sugar]

❶ Make a few shallow cuts on the sausages.
❷ Wash the potatoes. Without wiping them dry, place on a dish and heat, un-wrapped, in a microwave oven for about 5 minutes. Halfway through, turn over once. Peel and cut into 4 portions. Cut the lettuce into manageable pieces.
❸ Pour the tomatoes and liquid in a pot and coarsely crush. Add A and bring to a boil. Add the potatoes and sausages and

Tomato Soup with Sausage and Potato

adjust the seasoning with B. When all the ingredients have cooked down, add the lettuce. Eat as a soup.

Bouillon Soup with Gyoza and Chingensai

■ Ingredients (2 servings)

10 pieces   ready made frozen gyoza (p.79)

3 stocks   chingensai (bok choy with green stems)

1oz/30 g   harusame (bean threads)

½   negi (long onion)

A⌈ 600cc water, 1 Tbs sake, 1½ tsp
⌊ bouillon powder, ½ tsp salt, pinch of pepper

❶ Separate the chingensai into leaves and stalks and cut both into manageable sizes.

❷ Soak the harusame in boiling water until soft. Drain.

❸ Cut the long onion into thin diagonal slices.

❹ Heat A in a pot. When it comes to a boil, add all the ingredients. Serve the ingredients as they cook through.

Miso Soup with Long Onion and Tuna

■ Ingredients (2 servings)

7oz/200g   tuna, edible raw

1   negi (long onion)

3½oz/100g   shimeji mushrooms

600cc   dashi stock

1½ Tbs   miso and sake

❶ Cut the tuna into ⅜inch/1cm then rectangles.

❷ Cut the long onion into 1⅛inch/3cm lengths. Divide the shimeji into small clusters.

❸ Bring the dashi stock to a boil in a pot. Dissolve the miso and add to the dashi stock along with the sake. Add the long onion and simmer briefly. Add the fish and shimejis. Serve the ingredients as they cook through.

Wet the edges of the wrapper, fold and press to seal, making one pleat at the center.

Cheese Gyoza Soup

Cheese-filled bite-sized gyoza are rich and creamy. Serve hot from the pot.

15 min.
190 kcal

■ Ingredients (2 servings)
¼ onion
¾inch／2cm carrot
1 to 2 string beans (if available)
8 pieces round gyoza wrappers
1¾oz／50g processed cheese
1 Tbs butter
A ┌ 1 bouillon cube
  │ 400cc water
  └ 1 Tbs white wine
pinch of salt and pepper

❶ Cut the onion into ⅜-inch/1-cm-thick wedges. Cut the carrot into approx.⅓-inch/2-mm-thick pieces (you can use a vegetable cutter). Cut the string beans diagonally into ¾ to 1⅙-inch/2 to 3-cm-long thin slices.

❷ Cut the cheese into ⅜ inch/1 cm cubes. Cut the gyoza wrapper in half and wrap up the cheese to make a dumpling(see previous page).

❸ Melt the butter in a pot and sauté all the vegetables until the onion is tender. Add A and bring to a boil. Simmer for 2 to 3 minutes after boiling and add ②. When the gyoza wrappers are transparent, season with salt and pepper to taste.

Bean Soup

15 min.
196 kcal

Kintoki beans or Hiyoko beans can be substituted for kidney beans. Adding lemon juice at the end gives the recipe a refreshing flavor.

■ Ingredients (2 servings)
1 small can(5¼oz／150g) unseasoned kidney beans
¼ onion
4inch／10cm celery stalk
1 rasher bacon
½ Tbs vegetable oil

A ┌ 1 bouillon cube
  └ 400cc water
1 dried bay leaf
pinch of salt and pepper
½ Tbs lemon juice (optional)

❶ Thinly slice the onion. Diagonally cut the celery stalk into thin strips. Cut the bacon into ³⁄₁₆-inch/5-mm-wide pieces.

❷ Heat the oil in the pot and sauté the onion until tender. Add the celery and the bacon and continue to sauté.

❸ Add A, the kidney beans and the bay leaf. When boiled, skim off any scum and froth. Cover and simmer for about 10 minutes. Season with salt and pepper to taste. Serve with lemon juice, if preferred.

Miso Soup

Steamed rice and miso soup are a fundamental set menu in traditional Japanese meals. Miso soup is very easy to make, but it is a nutritionally balanced soup.

How to Make Instant Miso Soup

To start off, a very easy recipe using store-bought dashi powder is introduced, from which you can easily enjoy miso soup.

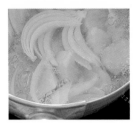  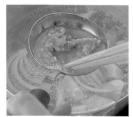

■ Ingredients (2 servings)

1 to 1½ Tbs   miso(p.96)

300cc   water

a few kinds of ingredients

1 to 2 tsp   dashi powder(p.96)

❶Put the ingredients in water in a pan and cook until tender. If the ingredients cook slowly and require a bit more time, add water to maintain the same amount.

❷When the ingredients are tender, add the dashi powder, following the instructions on the package.

❸Place the miso in a ladle and dissolve in a small amount of dashi stock from the pan. Pour back into the pan. When the soup boils again, remove from the heat and serve.

Ingredients
examples of very popular combinations

Littleneck Clams(Asari) Wash the clams well, rubbing the shells together. Put them in water in a pan and set over heat. When the clams open, skim off any froth. Dissolve the miso.

Corbicula Clams(Shigimi) See the recipe for "Littleneck Clams". If the taste is too light, add some dashi powder.

Onion and Potato Cut both ingredients into thin slices and cook until tender. Add the dashi powder and dissolve the miso.

Daikon Radish and Abura-age(p.96) Cut both ingredients into thin slices and cook until the daikon is tender. Add the dashi powder and dissolve the miso.

Miso Soup with Pork and Vegetables

■ Ingredients (2 servings)

1¾oz／50g···each thinly sliced pork flank, daikon radish,burdock and carrot／1···small potato／1···shiitake mushroom／¼···konnyaku jelly (p.96)／½Tbs···vegetable oil／1 to 2tsp···dashi powder／1 to 1½Tbs ···miso

❶ Shave the burdock and let soak in water. Blanch the konnyaku briefly and cut into thin slices.

❷ Cut the remaining ingredients into manageable sizes.

❸ Put the oil in a pan and sauté all the ingredients. Add 400cc of water and cook until the ingredients are tender. Add the dashi powder and dissolve the miso.

Miso Soup with Nagaimo

■ Ingredients (2 servings)

5¼oz／150g···nagaimo(Chinese yam)／aonori, powdered green laver (optional)／1 to 1½Tbs···miso／1 to 2tsp···dashi powder

❶ Peel the nagaimo and cut into ⅜-inch/1-cm-thick rounds, or into half-moon slices, if it is large.
❷ Put 300cc of water in a pan and cook until the nagaimo is tender.
❸ Add the dashi powder and dissolve the miso.
❹ Serve in a bowl and sprinkle with aonori, if available.

Dried Wakame and Potato
Soak the wakame in water for about 10 min. and cut into manageable pieces. Cook the potato until tender. Add the wakame and dashi powder and dissolve the miso.

Dried Wakame and Boiled Bamboo Shoot Do the same for the wakame as the left-hand recipe. Thinly slice the bamboo shoot. Place both in a pan of water. When it comes to a boil, add the dashi powder and dissolve the miso.

Tofu and Long Onion Cut the long onion into thin diagonal slices. Cut the tofu into thin slices. Place both in a saucepan of water and cook. When it comes to a boil, add the dashi powder and dissolve the miso.

Tofu and Nameko Mushrooms(or any other mushrooms) Wash the nameko very briefly. Cube the tofu. When it comes to a boil, add the dashi powder and dissolve the miso.

Mixed Mushroom Miso Soup

■ Ingredients (2 servings)

Small amount each of mushrooms such as shimeji, shiitake, maitake, etc./1 to 1½Tbs···miso／1 to 2tsp···dashi powder

❶ Remove the root clusters from the shimeji and divide into small bunches. Remove and discard the shiitake stems. Cut the shiitakes into ⅜-inch/1-cm-wide strips. Divide the maitake into small clusters.
❷ Put 300cc of water in a pan and cook all the mushrooms very briefly. Add the dashi powder and dissolve the miso.
❸ Sprinkle with 7-spice pepper or sansho(Japanese pepper) powder to enhance the flavor, if desired.

Beef and Daikon Soup

20 min.
202 kcal

Using meat with moderate fat gives a more delicious finish. As this is a rather rich and heavy dish, you are recommended to serve this when the main dish is light.

Carefully skimming off any scum and froth is the key to making a clear, tasty broth.

■ Ingredients (2 servings)

3½oz／100g　　beef, thinly sliced
1½inch／4cm(5¼oz／150g) daikon radish
⅙oz／5g　　ginger
4inch／10cm　negi (long onion)
⅓oz／10g　　harusame(bean threads)
½ Tbs　　sesame oil

A ⎡ 1　　bouillon cube
　 ⎣ 500cc　　water

B ⎡ 1 Tbs　　sake
　 ⎣ 1 tsp　　soy sauce

❶ Soak the harusame in boiling water until tender and cut into 2 inch/5cm lengths. Cut the daikon into 1½-inch/4-cm-long thin rectangles. Thinly slice the ginger. Cut the long onion into thin diagonal slices. Cut the meat into 1⅙-inch/3-cm-wide pieces.

❷ Heat the sesame oil in a pan and sauté the ginger, meat and daikon.

❸ When the meat turns whitish, add A and bring to a boil. Skim off any scum and froth.

❹ When the daikon is tender, add the harusame. Season with B to taste and add the long onion just before removing from heat.

■ Ingredients (2 servings)

1 (5¼oz/150g) potato

½ negi (long onion)

½ tomato

½ Tbs butter

A ⌈1 bouillon cube
  ⌊400cc water

pinch of salt and pepper

pinch of minced parsley

❶ Peel and cut the potato into ³⁄₁₆-inch/5-mm-thick quarter-rounds. Cut the long onion into ³⁄₈-inch/1-cm-thick round slices. Seed the tomato and cut into large pieces.

❷ Set a pan over low heat, melt the butter and sauté the long onion until tender. Add the potato

Potato and Long Onion Soup

15 min.
105 kcal

and continue to sauté.

❸ Add A and the tomato and turn up the heat to high. When it comes to a boil, reduce the heat to moderate and simmer for about 10 minutes until just before the potato crumbles. Adjust the seasoning with salt and pepper. Serve in a bowl and sprinkle with minced parsley.

■ Ingredients (2 servings)

7oz/200g hamaguri(hard-shell clams), any sand removed

5 to 6 watercress

A ⌈½ tsp bouillon powder
  │300cc water
  ⌊1 Tbs sake

pinch of salt and pepper

❶ Wash the hamaguri well by rubbing the shells together. Cut the watercress into 1½inch/4 cm lengths.

❷ Put A and the clams in a pan and set over heat. When the clam shells open, skim off any froth and season with salt and pepper to taste.

❸ Add the watercress and remove from heat.

Clam and Watercress Soup

The ingredients used in this recipe go well with broth made from chicken bone or kombu kelp instead of bouillon powder. Choose the broth depending upon the main dish.

5 min.
25 kcal

![icon] **5 min. 80 kcal** ▶ # Tofu and Egg Puff Soup

This soup uses an egg-tofu mixture, which creates a light, fluffy texture, different from soup which contains only egg or only tofu.

■ Ingredients (2 servings)

⅓ block (3½oz／100g) "silk" tofu(p.96)

1 egg

1 to 2 scallions

A ⎡ 1 tsp bouillon powder
　 ⎣ 400cc water

pinch of salt and sesame oil

❶ Cut the scallions into fine rings. Put A in a pan and set over heat.

❷ Crush the tofu in a bowl, add the egg and mix well.

❸ When A has boiled, drizzle with ② and simmer for 1 to 2 minutes without stirring until the mixture of the tofu and egg comes up to the surface.

❹ Season with salt to taste and sprinkle in sesame oil. Transfer to a bowl and sprinkle with scallions.

Using your hands is an easy and quick way to crush tofu. Sometimes hands can be a helpful and useful utensil.

■ Ingredients (2 servings)

5¼oz／150g asari (littleneck clams), any sand removed

3½oz／100g frozen mixed vegetables

½ Tbs butter

A ⌈1 bouillon cube
　⌊200cc water

200cc milk

50cc heavy cream

pinch of pepper

❶ Wash the clams well.

❷ Sauté the mixed vegetables in butter. Add A and simmer for about 1 minute after boiling.

❸ Add the clams and milk. When the clams open, add the heavy cream and adjust the seasoning with pepper.

Quick Clam Chowder

Note: You should soak the clams in salt water containing 1 tsp of salt per cup of water for about 30 minutes if possible, even though you bought "recipe-ready" clams.

5 min.
257 kcal

There are no ingredients to cut in this recipe. The cooking time is only 5 minutes, but produces a rich, full flavor!

Instant Clear Soup -Just add hot water-

These recipes are helpful friends when you want to add a soup to the menu, but you don't have much preparation time. The key is to combine ingredients that have a good taste with ingredients that have a good smell. After pouring hot water, adjust the seasoning with a pinch of salt and soy sauce.

Example Ingredients

chirimen-jako(p.96) wakame (p.96), cut into small pieces hanpen(soft fish cake)

salted kombu kelp mitsuba(p.96) ground sansho(Japanese pepper)

Tororo-kombu(wafer-thin kombu kelp) umeboshi(p.96) negi(long onion)

dried bonito flakes(p.96) yaki-nori(p.96) okra

kombu kelp tea scallions enoki mushrooms

Fried Rice with Okaka*
*Dried bonito flakes(p.96)

Serve with several varieties of unbattered fried seasonal vegetables as a garnish to make a well-balanced dish.

5 min.
412 kcal

■ Ingredients (2 servings)
10½oz／300g   hot steamed rice
⅓oz／10g   dried bonito flakes
1 Tbs   butter
1-odd Tbs   soy sauce
½ sheet   yaki-nori(p.96)

❶ Melt the butter in a skillet and stir-fry the rice over high heat until the grains separate completely.

❷ Add the bonito flakes and mix. Pour the soy sauce around the edge of the skillet and stir once.

❸ Transfer to a plate and sprinkle with the yaki-nori.

Note: The key to this recipe is to quickly stir-fry over high heat. Woks (Chinese frying pans with 2 loop handles or one long handle and with a rounded base) are the best pans for cooking fried rice.

Deep-fry 3½oz／100g of pumpkin, 3 bell peppers and 2 eggplants(unbattered). Sprinkle with a pinch of salt and pepper.

Fried Rice with Oyster Sauce

This recipe has a flavor like Chinese chimaki(rice-dumplings wrapped in bamboo leaves). Don't be afraid to use lots of perilla leaves, as they have a refreshing taste.

10 min.
451 kcal

■ Ingredients (2 servings)
14oz／400g   hot steamed rice
1 Tbs   vegetable oil
2⅘oz／80g   roast pork
10 to 20   perilla leaves(p.96)
1½ Tbs   oyster sauce

❶ Cut the roast pork into ⅜inch／1cm cubes. Cut the perilla leaves into about ⅐-inch／4-mm-wide pieces. Soak in water until crisp and drain.

❷ Heat the oil in a skillet and stir-fry the rice over high heat until all of it is coated with oil. Add the roast pork and continue stir-frying until the rice grains separate completely.

❸ Pour the oyster sauce around the edge of the skillet and stir once. Remove and mix with the perilla leaves.

| 10 min. |
| 374 kcal |

Scallop and Agedama Bowl

This recipe can be handily made using agedama sold in the market, which has a ten-don flavor.

Ten-don is a bowl of rice with tempura** on top.

■ Ingredients (2 servings)

10½oz／300g hot steamed rice

6　　　　scallops,edible raw

6 pieces　　mitsuba(p.96)

4 Tbs　　　agedama*

A ⎡70cc　　　dashi stock
  ⎢1 Tbs　　　soy sauce
  ⎣1 Tbs　　　mirin

¼ sheet　　yaki-nori (P.96),
　　　　　　　thinly sliced

❶ Cut the scallop in half cross-wise. Cut the mitsuba into ¾ inch／2cm lengths.

❷ Combine A in a pan and set over heat. When boiled, add the scallop and cook until the surface is opaque. Add the agedama and cook for about 1 minute. Remove from heat and sprinkle with mitsuba.

❸ Top ② on the rice in a bowl and serve with the yaki-nori.

*Agedama are the batter dregs left over after making tempura.

**Tenpura is a kind of Japanese deep-fry, in which fresh ingredients such as seafood or vegetables are lightly battered and deep-fried.

To make varieties of this recipe, add onion to the ingredients or drizzle an egg over the ingredients.

■ Ingredients(2 servings)

14oz／400g   hot steamed rice

3½oz／100g   tuna, edible raw

½ tsp   wasabi paste(p.96)

1 Tbs   soy sauce

1 small pack (approx.1oz／30g)
    natto (p.96)

⅔oz／20g   takuan(p.96)

½ sheet   yaki-nori(p.96)

2   scallions

❶ Mix the wasabi paste and soy sauce. Cut the tuna into ⅜inch／1cm cubes and coat with the wasabi-soy mixture.

❷ Cut the takuan into ⅜inch／5 mm cubes and the scallions into thin rings.

❸ Place a portion of hot steamed

Tuna and Natto Bowl

Several kinds of traditional Japanese ingredients are used in this recipe. The combination of smooth, moist natto and crunchy takuan produces a unique texture.

rice in a bowl. Crumple up the yaki-nori and top on the rice. Lay ①, ② and the natto on top. Sprinkle with a little soy sauce, if desired.

Beef and Soybean Sprouts on Rice

This is an instant rice bowl similar to the famous Korean bowl, Bibinba. Be careful not to let the soybean sprouts overcook.

■ Ingredients (2 servings)

14oz／400g   hot steamed rice

5¼oz／150g   beef shoulder,
                thinly sliced

A ⎡1 Tbs   soy sauce and sake
  ⎢½ Tbs   sesame oil
  ⎣⅓oz／10g   garlic, grated

5¼oz／150g soybean sprouts

1 Tbs   vegetable oil

B [½Tbs sugar and soy sauce]

1 Tbs   roasted sesame seeds

❶ Cut the meat into ⅜-inch／1-cm-wide pieces and mix well with A. Allow to marinate.

❷ Heat the oil in a skillet and sauté ① until heated through. Add the soybean sprouts and briefly sauté over high heat.

❸ Combine B, and add to ②, stirring once. Add the sesame and mix again.

❹ Put the rice in a bowl and lay ③ on top.

■ Ingredients (2 servings)

10½oz/300g hot steamed rice
2⅘oz/80g beef loin,thinly sliced
1⅖oz/40g carrot
2 shiitake mushrooms
1oz/30g nira (p.96)

A
- 1 bouillon cube
- 600cc water
- 1 tsp soy sauce

B
- ⅕ tsp salt
- pinch of pepper

❶ Cut the carrot into thin quarter rounds. Cut the shiitakes into diagonal slices and the nira into 1⅙inch/3cm lengths. Cut the meat into 1⅙-inch/3-cm-wide pieces.
❷ Put A in a pan and set over heat. When boiled, add the meat, carrot and shiitakes and skim off any scum and froth. Season with B to taste and add the nira. When it comes to a boil, remove.
❸ Put the rice in a serving bowl and pour the hot ② over the rice.

8 min.
329 kcal

Rice Soup

Make a soup with all the ingredients while heating left-over rice in a microwave oven, and you can serve this hot dish in no time.

Ingredients (2 servings)

5¼oz／150g	steamed rice
5¼oz／150g	frozen mixed seafood
1	ripened tomato
⅙oz／5g	garlic, minced
1 tsp	vegetable oil

A ⌈ 200cc water
  │ 1 tsp bouillon powder
  └ ¼ tsp curry powder

pinch of salt and pepper
pinch of minced parsley

❶ Cut the tomato into ½inch／1½cm cubes.

❷ Heat the oil in a pan and sauté the garlic over low heat. When the flavor is released, turn up the heat and briefly sauté the tomato. Add A.

Seafood Risotto

15 min.
209 kcal

Curry powder is used to remove the fishy odor of the seafood.

❸ When boiled, add the rice and the mixed seafood. Simmer until it returns to a boil. Skim off any scum and froth, lower the heat and simmer for 3 to 4 minutes. Season with salt and pepper to taste. Transfer to a serving bowl and sprinkle with minced parsley.

Ingredients (2 servings)

5¼oz／150g hot steamed rice

A ⌈ pinch of salt and pepper
  └ ½ tsp bouillon powder

4	pieces ham
1¾oz／50g	pizza cheese
1	egg
2 Tbs	parsley, coarsely minced
2 Tbs	flour
2 Tbs	vegetable oil

❶ Mix A with the rice to season. Cut the ham into ⅜inch／1cm squares.

❷ Beat the egg. Add ①, the cheese, parsley and flour and mix together well.

Baked Flat Rice Cake

15 min.
435 kcal

❸ Heat 1 Tbs of vegetable oil in a skillet. Ladle out ⅙ of the batter into the skillet. Cook both sides until well browned.

Any ingredients you prefer will work for this recipe. Long onion, jako(dried young fish), or dried or steamed sakuraebi(tiny shrimp) are very good ingredients for a traditional Japanese flavored rice cake.

■ Ingredients (2 servings)

10 to 12 pieces   round gyoza
                wrappers, large size
½ Tbs   olive oil
2⅖oz／80g

    store-bought meat sauce
A ┌ 1¾oz／50g   mayonnaise
  └ 2 Tbs   milk or heavy cream
2 tsp   powdered cheese

❶ Bring water to a boil in a pan. Reduce the heat a little. Put the gyoza wrappers in the boiling water one by one. After about 10 seconds, plunge them into ice water. Immediately lift them out and spread them on a bamboo strainer without letting them touch each other.

❷ Spread the olive oil on a heat-proof dish. Place a gyoza wrapper open on the dish, lay about 1 tsp of the meat sauce on it and roll up. Let it slide to the other end of the dish. Do the same with the remaining wrappers .

❸ Combine A and pour it over ②. Sprinkle with cheese. Bake in a toaster oven for about 10 minutes until browned.

Home-Style Cannelloni

20 min.
408 kcal

You can make a great cannelloni-style dish, using round gyoza dumpling wrappers. Best served with wine.

(left) A skimmer can be used to take out the boiled gyoza wrappers.
(right) Make the cannelloni in a dish and then line them up before heating.

Ingredients (2 servings)

7oz／200g   cabbage

4   shiitake mushrooms

4   anchovies

A ⎡ 1   dried red pepper
   ⎣ ⅓oz／10g   garlic, minced

1 Tbs   olive oil

5⅗oz／160g   spaghetti

pinch of salt and pepper

❶ Boil the spaghetti as indicated on the package.

❷ Cut the red pepper in half and seed. Cut the cabbage and shiitakes into thin strips. Coarsely chop the anchovies.

❸ Heat the olive oil in a skillet and sauté A until aromatic. Add the cabbage and shiitakes and sauté until tender. Add the anchovies and stir together to coat.

Cabbage and Anchovy Pasta

15 min.
422 kcal

Season with salt and pepper.

❹ Ladle ③ on the boiled spaghetti.

Ingredients (2 servings)

3½oz／100g   shell pasta

2 pieces(1oz／30g)   ham

¼   onion

3 to 5   large basil leaves

1 Tbs   olive oil

A ⎡ 160cc   vegetable juice with a tomato base
   ⎢ 300cc   water
   ⎣ ½ tsp   bouillon powder

B [pinch of salt and pepper]

2oz／60g   cheese, a kind that melts well

❶ Cut the ham, onion and basil leaves (keep several for decoration) into ⅜inch/1cm squares.

❷ Sauté the onion until tender. Add the ham and pasta and briefly sauté. Add A and bring to a boil, then skim off any scum.

❸ Add the basil, cover and simmer over low heat until the pasta is tender. Adjust the seasoning with B.

❹ Remove from the heat. Add the cheese and stir once. Arrange the remaining basil leaves on top as a garnish.

Pasta in Vegetable Juice Sauce

15 min.
430 kcal

Rice Vermicelli Noodles in Soup

**15 min.
229 kcal**

■ Ingredients (2 servings)

1¾oz／50g		rice vermicelli noodles
1¾oz／50g		pork flank, thinly sliced
	pinch of salt and pepper	
1⅛inch／3cm		carrot
4inch／10cm		negi (long onion)
⅕oz／6g		dried shiitake mushrooms, thinly sliced
1oz／30g		bottled za cài (Chinese hot pickles)

A ⎰ 700cc — water
   ⎜ 1 — bouillon cube
   ⎜ 2 Tbs — sake
   ⎱ ½ Tbs — soy sauce

pinch of salt and pepper

Za cài is used as a hidden ingredient in this recipe. The cooking time is very short, making this recipe great to use.

❶ Cut the carrot into wafer-thin rectangles. Cut the long onion into thin diagonal slices.

❷ Cut the meat into manageable sizes and sprinkle with salt and pepper.

❸ Soak the rice vermicelli noodles in boiling water and cut into manageable lengths.

❹ Put A in a pan and bring to a boil. Add the meat and skim off any scum. Add the shiitakes, carrot and za cài and simmer until the carrot is tender. Add the rice vermicelli noodles and long onion and adjust the seasoning with salt and pepper.

1 to 2 minutes(in boiling water) is sufficient soaking time for the rice vermicelli noodles, so as not to length-en and soften them too much.

■ Ingredients (2 servings)

3½oz／100g   nira(P.96)

A ⎡ 130cc   1 egg + water
  ｜ 1 cup   flour
  ⎣ pinch of salt and pepper

1 Tbs   vegetable oil

<dip>

1 tsp   rice vinegar

½ tsp   soy sauce

pinch of là yŏu (Chinese chile oil)

pinch of sugar

❶ Cut the nira into approx.2 inch/5cm lengths. Combine A, mix and add the nira.

❷ Heat ½ Tbs of oil in a skillet. Slide in half the amount of the batter, flatten it and pan-broil over moderate heat until browned.

Korean Okonomiyaki

20 min. 300 Kcal

Turn over and continue to cook the other side until nicely browned, smoothing down the top with a turner. Do the same for the remaining batter.

❸ Combine the ingredients for the dip and use to dress the pancake.

Quick Steamed Raisin Bread

Orange juice or yogurt is a good substitute for milk.

2 min. 122 kcal

■ Ingredients (for 1 bread)

4 Tbs   store-bought pancake mix

2 Tbs   milk

About 10   dried raisins

❶ Put the pancake mix and milk in a cup and mix well. Add the raisins* and mix.

❷ Loosely wrap the cup and heat in a microwave oven for about 1 minute(2 minutes for 2 cups).**

*Approx. ⅓inch/8mm diced both ½ piece of ham and ⅓oz／10g of cheese can be substituted for raisins.

**The heating time will differ a little depending on how large or how thick the cup is. Heat for about 1 minute, then check. If the batter is still sticky, heat for 10 seconds at a time until the batter near the edge of the cup is dry and the bread is done.

Japanese Ingredients Used in This Book

―Available at ordinary supermarkets―

Japanese name is in [ ].

Soy Sauce   **[Miso]**   **Sake**   **Rice Vinegar**

[Syoyu]   [Nihon-shu]   [Su]

These are the essential seasonings for everyday Japanese cooking, so keep them handy. Soy sauce and miso are made from soybeans, and sake and rice vinegar from rice.

[Mirin], or sweet cooking rice wine gives a sweet taste and glossy finish to dishes. The sweetness of mirin is milder and deeper than that of sugar. Sake sweetened with sugar(ratio 3:1)can be substituted.

① ②

①**Dried Bonito Flakes** [Kezuri-katsuo]

②**Instant Dasi Stock** [Dashi-no-moto]

Dashi is a basic ingredient in Japanese cuisine. ①〜④ are typical ingredients for making dashi stock. Soak in cold water or add to boiling water to draw the flavor-rich ingredients from them. ① is usually used to make dashi stock. Steam the bonito fillet, dry well, and then shave into flakes. ② is added to boiling water. Very convenient for making small amounts.

⑤ ⑥

⑤**7-spice Pepper**[Shichimi-togarashi]
This traditional Japanese seasoning has a spicy, rich flavor.

⑥**Wasabi Paste**[Neri-wasabi]
This light green paste is made from grated wasabi root. It is commonly sold in a tube.

⑤ and ⑥ are frequently used at the table.

Mushrooms[Kinoko]

Clockwise from left:
[Maitake]   **[Eringi]**   **[Shimeji]**
[Enoki]   **[Nameko]**   **[Shiitake]**
All mushrooms except nameko can be substituted for each other.

③**Dried Kelp**[Kombu]   ④**[Niboshi]**

When using ③, wipe lightly, leaving the white powder which adds flavor. ④ are small sun-dried sardines.

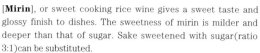

Long Onion[Negi]   **[Banno-negi]**   **Burdock Root**[Gobo]

[Yuzu]
     [Sudachi]

[Kabosu]

These citron family fruits have mild sourness, and should be used seasonally. They can be substituted with lemon or lime.

Perilla Leaves
[Shiso]

[Nira]
variety of leek

[Myoga]
Ginger

Trefoil[Mistuba]

These ⑮〜⑲ are served with the traditional Japanese breakfast. They have been quite popular as reserve foods as well.

⑮**[Yaki-nori]**   ⑯**[Umeboshi]**
Toasted laver

Can be eaten as is. Store in an air-tight container in a dry place.

These pickled Japanese plums are a very sour, alkaline food.

⑦  ⑧   ⑨

[Tofu]

⑩   ⑪

⑦**"Cotton" Tofu**[Momen-tofu]
⑧**"Silk" Tofu**[Kinugoshi-tofu]
⑨**Grilled Tofu**[Yaki-tofu]
⑩**Thin Deep-fried Tofu**[Abura-age]
⑪**Thick Deep-fried Tofu**[Atsu-age]

Tofu is made by curdling the juice squeezed from soybeans. ⑦ has a rough surface and firm texture. ⑧ is much smoother. ⑨ is broiled ⑦. Before using ⑩ or ⑪, pour hot water over it to remove excess oil.

⑫  ⑬

⑭

⑫ ⑬**Konnyaku Jelly**[Konnyaku]
These are calorie-free but rich in glycomannan. Brown and white konnyaku are different only in color.

⑭**[Shirataki]**   This type of konnyaku is cut into long white threads.

Dried Wakame Seaweed[Wakame]   **Dried Hijiki Seaweed**[Hijiki]

⑰**[Chirimen-jako]**
Dried young fish. The best quality is small and uniform in size.

⑱**[Takuan]**
Pickled daikon radish

⑲**[Natto]**
Prepared fermented soybeans